PRODUCING MUSIC WITH ABLETON LIVE

quick PRO guides

Producing Music with Ableton Live

Jake Perrine

Hal Leonard Books

An Imprint of Hal Leonard Corporation

Published in 2012 by Hal Leonard Books
An Imprint of Hal Leonard Corporation
7777 West Bluemound Road
Milwaukee, WI 53213

Trade Book Division Editorial Offices
33 Plymouth St., Montclair, NJ 07042

Book design by Adam Fulrath
Book composition by Bill Gibson

Library of Congress Cataloging-in-Publication Data
Perrine, Jake.
  Producing music with Ableton Live / Jake Perrine.
      p. cm.
  1. Ableton Live. 2. Digital audio editors. I. Title.
  ML74.4.A23P47 2011
  781.3'4536–dc23
                                    2011029813

Printed in the United States of America

ISBN 978-1-4584-0036-9

www.halleonardbooks.com

CONTENTS

Chapter 3

Chapter 4

Chapter 5

Chapter 6

Chapter 7

Chapter 8

INTRODUCTION

Mission

I know the feeling. Symphonies of sound flow through you. If only you had a way to express the rivers of vibration that only you can hear in your head! The size, the impact, the dynamic range, the subtlety, the grandeur, the raw emotion, and the unique blend of timbres that makes you . . . you!

It can be frustrating harboring a wellspring of inspiration with no means to share your unique voice. So, like millions before you, you decide to undertake a lifelong journey: you seek out a point on the horizon that will take you to your goal. Like a painter picking up a paintbrush, you search for the tools that will enable your expression. And that is what has led you to this book. Well done. As Obi-Wan Kenobi once wisely said to Luke, "You have just taken your first step into a larger world."

And while this decision to learn a craft is an important step—perhaps the most important step—it is by no means the first step: you have known music and sound all your life, and you've spent countless hours formulating melodies, beats, lyrics, soundscapes, rises and falls, builds and breakdowns, at times to the exclusion of any other thought or activity. This wealth of experience is infinitely valuable. It is the palette of colors that you will draw your inspiration from. Hold onto that. Feed it. Nurture it. Treat it with the utmost respect. Your song is unique in all the universe.

And if you are just starting, there is good news! There has never been a better time to get into electronic-music creation. Never before in the short history of electronic music making have the tools been so powerful, available, inexpensive, and easy to use. Gone are the days of splicing tape and rooms full of gear. With a laptop and some headphones, you can make world-class-caliber music wherever and whenever the inspiration strikes.

There are many different music applications available to choose from. You've made an excellent choice in selecting Ableton Live! I am not shy about my passion for this program—you'll find it on every page of this book—and I hope to inspire the same passion in you. In my humble opinion, Ableton Live represents the best know-how of more than a century of electronic-music makers. It does some very powerful things simply and gracefully in a streamlined interface that is easy to learn, easy to use, and enjoyable to work with.

On the surface, there are many similarities between Live and other multitrack recording and editing packages. Live will definitely do a majority of what those programs can. But in addition to all that standard functionality, Live really shines in its additional ability to work with audio on the fly, or "live." As its name implies, it was built with live performance in mind, and in this regard, no other program even comes close.

Another aspect of Live that impresses me is its versatility. Often there are many ways to accomplish similar results within Live, and instead of being locked into one way of doing things, Live's simple yet flexible design allows people to create in their own way. And because there are so many ways to combine Live's features, people are continually discovering new things to do with it! I've used it for composing, arranging, scoring, jamming with other musicians, remixing, DJ'ing, doing live Looping, art installations, teaching music theory, and sound design for theater, dance, film and videogames. I'm sure there are many more uses I've not yet tried.

Add to that an avid community of users who love to exchange ideas, tips, and techniques! In all my years of music making, I've never seen a group of users so fanatic about a product or as open about sharing what they know with other users. It really is a true community endeavor. Have a question? Jump on the Ableton forum. Wonder how somebody made that sound? Look it up on YouTube. Looking for a new way to DJ your tunes to a crowd? Download another user's templates and controller mappings they've created. You could spend all your waking hours exploring the wealth of materials available online—believe me, I've tried—and you would have hardly scratched the surface.

So let's get started!

How to Use This Book

The concepts in this book continue in the companion book Sound Design, Mixing, and Mastering with Ableton Live, and that book picks up right where this one leaves off with very little overlap. Although both books were created to stand on their own, they work best when used together.

The goal of this book is not to explain to you every single feature of the program. You already have Ableton's excellent reference manual for that. The goal is to get you making music quickly as possible using the key features that you will use every day, learning specific techniques that will help you reach your goals. When you are ready to delve more deeply, the second book will take you through the remaining, more complex aspects of the program.

If you are just getting started, I recommend moving through this book in a linear fashion. The lessons are sequential, building a song from the ground up, as you learn about Live's features in a hands-on fashion. Each new lesson builds upon the techniques discussed in previous chapters, referencing the previous terms and techniques discussed there. However, if you already have some experience with the program, you can jump in where it feels appropriate, as each exercise has its own corresponding Live Set to get you started at that point.

Appendices

One feature of these books I am excited to bring to you is that of the appendices. These topics are isolated from the rest of the book because they cover subjects that will be referenced throughout the lessons, and I did not want to impede the focus of the exercises with a bunch of sidebars. If you are unclear about one of the appendix topics referenced in a lesson, take the time to study it.

However, I've included these appendix topics for another important reason. For more than a decade I have taught audio production concepts, including MIDI, sound design, and Ableton Live to budding new audio engineers. Professional audio engineers make it their job to understand a wide array of concepts, because their careers depend upon it. But in the past decade, I have seen a massive influx of what I like to refer to as "The Laptop Producer." This is someone, perhaps like yourself, who does not aim to sit in a studio behind a console recording and mixing bands, but rather wants to use their laptop and perhaps a few controllers to make their own music. Laptop Producers do not need to now how to calibrate a 2-inch analog tape machine, but there are a few key audio-related concepts that do affect them that they often have no knowledge about. I get asked questions about these topics, such as frequency and amplitude or sample rate and bit depth, all the time, and while there is a lot of information online about such topics, there is even more misinformation about them So, the appendices are a subset of topics that are not necessarily Ableton Live specific, but will greatly aid you in working with the program and making computer music in general. I have intentionally tried to give you enough depth in these topics so that you can work with them confidently and not be bogged down in a lot of technical detail that won't serve your needs.

Supplemental Content

Included with this book is a DVD-ROM of materials that we will be using as a basis for many of the exercises herein. Copy the entire Book Content folder from the DVD-ROM to your hard drive before starting the exercises. (See appendix G for more information.)

The Book Content folder contains three subfolders:

- **Exercise Sets**—This folder contains a series of Live Sets that are the starting point for each exercise in the book, so you can jump in wherever you like.
- **Install**—This folder contains some of my favorite third-party plug-ins. Some of the plug-ins are freeware that you can use for free indefinitely, and some of them are demo versions that will expire after a trial period unless you purchase them. These plug-ins are described in appendix G.
- **Sounds to Sample**—Our friends over at **SoundsToSample.com** have provided a great collection of raw audio materials that you will use to construct the included exercises. If you like what you hear, head over to their website and check out their comprehensive supply of loops and samples for sale. I have yet to find another site that has as much quality to choose from with such a user-friendly interface. Highly recommended!

Assumptions

This book makes a few basic assumptions that are worth mentioning beforehand so that we are all on the same page. They include the following.

Basic Computer Experience

Making music with computers is not rocket science, but neither is it as easy as surfing the web or writing a letter in a word-processing program. That you are interested in pushing your computer and your creativity to higher levels leads me to believe that you feel some basic level of comfort with things like hooking up your computer, installing applications, saving files to a hard drive, navigating through folders, and so on. Even better if you have a bit of experience troubleshooting your computer, because periodically things inevitably don't function the way you expect them to, especially when you are pushing your computer to its limits making music. If these kinds of tasks seem overly challenging or beyond your level of computer experience, you may want to spend some time obtaining some basic computing skills before moving on to digital audio wrangling. There are a plethora of schools, books, and online tutorials for just this sort of thing.

Understanding of Basic Music Terminology

While I don't expect that you have necessarily had lots of music theory training, I do expect that you will understand basic musical terminology such as bars, beats, octaves, tempo, time signature, quarter notes, 16th notes, and the like. If this kind of language seems foreign to you, you can still make it through this book, but knowing the basics of music will help you to not only understand this material but also communicate with other musicians. I encourage you to seek out this understanding either through books, school, private tutoring, or the Internet.

Versions of Live

For the purposes of this book, I will assume that you are using the full version of Ableton Live—the current latest version of the program—but that is not a requirement. You can happily enjoy a vast majority of this instruction using a previous version of the program, because many of the core concepts remain the same.

The same can be said of Ableton Live Intro, the highly affordable feature-limited version of Live. You may run into some limitations of Intro while using this book, but the majority of the concepts are very much applicable.

As well, while I may make an occasional reference to Ableton Live Suite 8—the fullest version of the program that additionally includes a sizeable library of Instrument Devices and Presets—the Suite is not required in order to use this book.

Optional Useful Audio Gear

You need no other gear besides a computer and a copy of Live to make music or complete most of the book's exercises. However, appendix E, "The Makings of a Producer's Studio," will give you some ideas for future expansion. Here is a short list of optional gear that would be useful to have when working with Live, and this book, in order of importance:

- A pair of quality, closed-ear headphones—Closed-ear headphones surround the ear, giving better sound isolation and a far better sound than earbuds and the like. If you can't hear the sounds that you are making in detail, you have no way of knowing if what you are doing sounds good. Sony MDR7506 headphones cost about $100 and are my personal favorites over other headphones costing many times more.
- A USB keyboard controller—This is an external USB controller with keys and/or drum pads for playing in notes, with sliders and knobs for adjusting parameters. Novation and Akai make some great controllers for $200 to $500.
- A USB or FireWire audio interface with MIDI I/O, and two powered near-field studio monitors—Headphones are fine for getting started, but if you are serious about learning how to mix audio proficiently, you will need a way to get quality audio out of your computer and moving through the air via studio monitors. A wide range of these monitors are available today, and generally you get what you pay for, so try not to skimp on these when you decide to buy. An entry-level audio interface will cost from $150 to $500, and a basic pair of studio monitors will run from about $200 to $1,000.

Caution: If making computer music is your passion, you will find that once you get on the gear-purchasing escalator it is very hard to get off, so be prepared for addiction!

Conventions

What follows is a list of the shorthand conventions used in this book. Keeping these conventions streamlined and consistent will allow you to move smoothly and quickly through the exercises.

Keyboard Shortcuts

I am a keyboard shortcut fanatic! In Live, there are typically multiple ways of doing most tasks. I will list them all, but you will note that I always put the keyboard shortcut first. I heartily encourage you to try to commit to memory the keyboard shortcut as quickly as possible. Write it down if that helps you, or keep Ableton's own keyboard shortcut list open in another window so that you can refer to it as needed. I like to try to commit to learning one new shortcut each time I sit down in front of a program. If it is a program you work with regularly, you will learn them quickly and steadily. You might ask, "Why learn shortcuts?" One very simple answer: speed. The more keyboard shortcuts you know, the faster you can work. The faster you can work, the faster you can translate the idea in your head to something you—and everyone else—can hear.

I will always write out the keyboard shortcuts in the following format:
[(Macintosh modifier key)-(key)/(Windows modifier key)-(key)]

And I will be abbreviating the modifier keys like so:

- ctrl = Control (Macintosh and Windows)
- opt = Option (Macintosh)
- alt = Alternate (Windows)
- cmd = Command (Macintosh)
- shift = Shift (Macintosh and Windows)

So, when I write the following command:
"To save your session use [cmd-s/ctrl-s]",

This means "Use [Command and "s"] on the Macintosh, or [Control and "s"] on Windows."

If the keyboard shortcut is the same on both platforms, I will use only one command. For example:

"Press [spacebar] to begin playback."

This means that the spacebar will begin playback on both Mac and PC.

Menu Items

I also have a shorthand for executing menu commands, and it looks like this:

• Go File > Save.

This simply means, "Click on the File menu, and in that menu click on the Save function." If there is a further submenu, it might look like this:

• Go Edit > Record Quantization > Sixteenth-Note Quantization.

This simply indicates, "Click on the Edit menu, scroll down to the Record Quantization submenu item, and then select Sixteenth-Note Quantization." Easy!

Control-Click/Right-Click

Often PC mice will have a right-click button in addition to the standard left-click button. Some Mac mice do as well, but a lot of them don't. In Live (and in a lot of other apps) on Mac, the equivalent to a right-click is a Control-click (holding down the Control button while clicking on something). To indicate this gesture I will use a convention similar to keyboard shortcuts:

• [Ctrl-click/right-click]

This means "On a Mac, hold down Control and click, or on a PC, click on the right mouse button."

Do It! When you see this heading, there is a task or series of tasks that I am asking you to try out. Not every one of these is essential to complete before moving on to the next task, but the majority are, so as the sign says, do it!

Important! This heading indicates a key concept that you should pay special attention to before moving on.

Cool! These asides are little tidbits of geekery that are typically for fun and impressing friends with your trivia knowledge! I've thrown these in to add a little color and context to what you are learning.

Chapter 1
THE ABLETON LIVE INTERFACE

I know you are eager to make some sound. But before jumping into making some music, we should have a look around at the various parts of the Live interface and get familiar with them.

Cool! The graphic interface of Live was designed from the start to be easy to look at for long hours and for your computer to display quickly, which becomes increasingly important when you are working on a complex song or mixing a Set live, pushing your computer to its limits. The simpler the interface graphics, the less time and processor power your computer spends rendering the interface, and the more power it has left over to create high-quality audio. And if you don't like the classic default black-on-gray color scheme, you can simply jump into Live's Preferences to radically change it.

The Two Views: Session and Arrangement

The first feature I'd like to introduce you to in Live is not only its most important feature but also the one that sets it apart from all other audio programs: its two different views. If you just opened Live, you are currently looking at what is called Session View. Before we learn about Session View, let's visit the other view, Arrangement View, and learn our first keyboard shortcut.

Do It! Here are three ways to switch between Session View and Arrangement View:

- Press the [tab] key on your keyboard.
- Go View > Arrangement or View > Session.
- Click on one of the View selection buttons.

Pic. 1a: The two View selection buttons.

Repeat one of the above to switch back and forth as needed.

The relationship between these two views is the heart and soul of Ableton Live's power, and we will explore it in detail. Essentially, the two views offer two ways of interacting with your music. For now, just note the parts of the interface that change (the center area) and the parts that stay the same (the rest) when switching between the views.

Cool! Did you notice that Ableton's company logo is made out of the Session View and Arrangement View Selector buttons? That should give you an idea of how central these two views are to using Live!

The Session View Interface

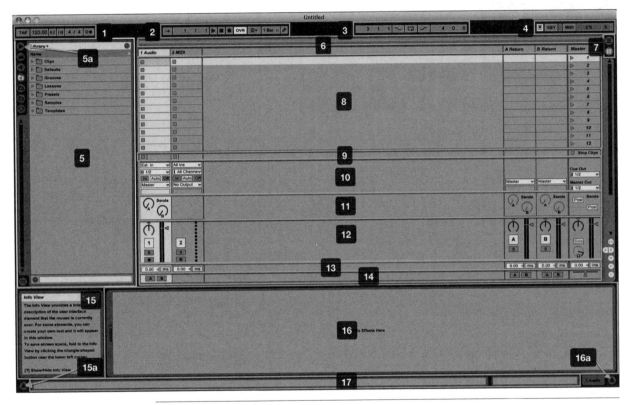

Pic. 1b: Session View areas.

When you first launch the program, you are looking at a blank Session View. Session View is made up of the following areas:

- 1. The Tempo and Time Signature controls
- 2. The Transport controls
- 3. The Arrangement Loop controls
- 4. The Keyboard/MIDI mapping controls and the CPU/Disk Activity Meter
- 5. The Browser and (5a) the Browser Show/Hide button
- 6. The Overview
- 7. The View Selector
- 8. The Session View Clip Slot Grid and Scene Slots
- 9. The Track Status Display and Stop All Clips button
- 10. The In/Out section

- · 11. The Sends section
- · 12. The Mixer
- · 13. The Track Delay section
- · 14. The Crossfader section
- · 15. The Info View area and (15a) the Info View Show/Hide button
- · 16. The Detail View area and (16a) the Detail View Show/Hide button
- · 17. The Status Bar

Cool! Many of the dividers between areas can be moved, thereby resizing their bordering areas. For example, click-and-drag the black vertical divider between the Browser area and the main Session View Clips grid to the left and right. Try the same thing, but vertically this time, on the divider between the Mixer and the Detail View area. You can make an area larger or smaller as your focus changes. Nice!

We'll go through each of these areas and a few more as they come up. For now just note their names and locations. Note as well that many of these areas can be hidden from view to make more room for the parts of the interface that you are currently using.

Do It! Here are three ways to show or hide many of these areas:

- · Use a keyboard shortcut (all of which are shown in the View menu).
- · Click on the appropriate Show/Hide button on the interface.
- · Go View > (the area you wish to Show/Hide).

Cool! One area you might want to keep open all the time while you are learning the program is the Info View located in the lower left corner. This area will give you a brief description of any item you roll your cursor over, and will often tell you the keyboard shortcut for that item as well. The keyboard shortcut for Show/Hide Info View is, not surprisingly, the question mark [?], also known as [shift-/]. Turn it on, and leave it on!

An Introduction to Live Projects and Live Sets

Pop quiz: What is the most important keyboard shortcut of all?

Answer: [Cmd-s/ctrl-s], which saves your work!

Let's take a moment to understand how Live handles the important tasks of saving and organizing your work using two important concepts: Live Projects and Live Sets.

- · A Live Set contains the work you do in Live, much the way a text file is a collection of the typing you do in a text editor. It is typically named with the .als extension when saving.
- · A Live Project is a folder that contains one or more Live Set files and a series of folders and files referenced by those Sets. This includes the Samples folder, which contains any recordings made in that Project.

Think of it this way: When you make a song, you may want to make multiple versions of that song: different arrangements, different tempos, or even multiple remixes. Each of those versions could be a different Live Set. Live also assumes that you would likely want all the different versions of that song together in a single place, as they likely would share some of the same recordings (perhaps the vocal takes are the same for all versions of the song, even if different combinations of them are used in each version). The Live Project is a folder containing all of the versions of your song and some of the audio elements common to all the Sets.

A typical Live Project folder may contain the following:

- Ableton Project Info (folder)—Live uses files in this folder to keep track of settings for the Project. You should not delete, move or rename this folder for any reason. Leave it as it is.
- The Live Set (file with the extension .als)—One or more Live Sets you have created in this Project.
- Samples folder—This folder is where Live keeps the various media that you create while working on your Set. We'll get into details about this folder and its usage later.

Important! Although the Live Set plays back audio, the Live Set file (.als) does not contain any audio itself! If you look at the size of the Live Set file, you will see that it has a relatively small file size compared to most audio files. The Live Set references other audio files on your hard drive, some of which may be in the Project folder's Samples folder.

When Live first opens, it creates a new, blank Set. This Set is not yet saved, and as such exists only in a temporary folder until you save it. I find it a very good practice to immediately save the Set before you even get started working, so you can consciously choose where you want the saved files to live on your computer.

Do It! Let's get your Set and Project folders set up right:

1. Press [cmd-s/ctrl-s] or go File > Save Live Set.

When you hit the Save command for the first time in a new Set, you are presented with a standard Save File dialog box where you can name your file, choose a location, and click on the Save button.

2. Navigate to a sensible folder on your hard drive.
3. Name the Set "My Exercise" and be sure to note what folder you are saving to.
4. Click on Save.
5. Now, switch out of Live into your computer's standard file navigator (that is, Finder/Windows Explorer) and navigate to the location you just saved your Set to.

It should look something like this:

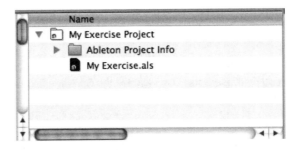

Pic. 1c: The Live Project folder and its contents (Mac).

Even though you issued a command to save the Live Set, note that what Live really saved was an entire Live Project folder that contains the Live Set as you named it. Live takes the liberty of naming your Project folder with the name of your Live Set, and adding the word "Project" on the end. So, the first time you save a Set, you actually save a Project that contains that Set. Note that there is not yet a Samples folder, because you have not yet added any audio to this Project.

6. Return to Live and go File > Save As… or press [cmd-shift-s/ctrl-shift-s].

Notice that you are now back inside the Project folder, where you see the current Live Set you saved previously.

7. Choose a new, similar name, such as My Exercise 1.als, and save it in the Project folder.

This time, Live does not save an entire new Project folder, rather just a second Live Set with a new name within the same Live Project folder. Perfect.

*   If you wanted to save your current Set as an entirely new Project, go File > Save As… and select a new location outside of the Project folder. Live will create a new Project based on the name you choose.
*   If you wanted to start an entirely new Project, you would go File > New Live Set [cmd-n/ctrl-n], and then save it as described above.

The Live Browser

As part of working with Live, you will find you regularly want to add a particular audio file, a plug-in, or some other file to your Set. Live has a very functional and convenient file browser built right into the program that offers a few key features to speed up your work flow. Let's have a look at it:

Do It! Here are three ways to Show/Hide the Live Browser:

*   Press [cmd-opt-b/ctrl-alt-b].
*   Click on the Show/Hide Browser Arrow button.
*   Go View > Browser > Show.

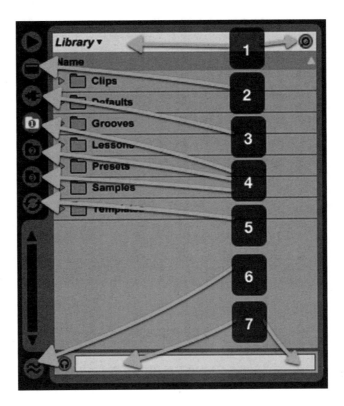

Pic. 1d: The Live Browser controls.

The Browser window has several buttons for accessing the various browsers and tools that you will want to familiarize yourself with:

1. The Bookmarks menu and Search button—Use the Search button to search your file system for files, Devices, or Presets. When using any of the three File Browsers below, this top area also becomes the Bookmarks pull-down menu. Use Bookmarks to quickly navigate to your regularly used hard-drive locations, such as the desktop and Live's Library. You can add a new bookmark to this list, such as a sample library or Projects drive, by navigating to a folder you want to bookmark and choosing Bookmark Current Folder from this pull-down menu.
2. The Live Device Browser—This area is a listing of Live's installed virtual Instruments, MIDI Effects, and Audio Effects for use in your Set. You will use this area a lot.
3. The Plug-in Device Browser—Here you will find a listing of your installed third-party (non-Ableton) plug-ins. This area may be empty if you do not own any of these Devices yet. If you install any of the third-party freeware or demo plug-ins that came with your book content, they will show up here when successfully installed. Be sure to close Live before installing new plug-ins.
4. File Browsers 1, 2, and 3—These are three file browsers for navigating your hard drive and network. Conveniently, they each remember where you last were browsing, so you can leave them set to three of your most used locations.
5. The Hot-Swap Browser—You will use this area to audition alternate Clips, Presets, Grooves, or samples for a given Device.
6. The Groove Pool Show/Hide button—This area is for choosing and working with Live's Groove templates.

7. The Preview tab—When previewing an audio file in the Browser, a small waveform overview will display in this box. Enable the headphones switch to automatically play a selected audio file through the Cue Out.

As you move through the exercises in the book, you will receive more detail about each of these browsers. For now, click on each of the browser buttons and scroll through what you find there to familiarize yourself with its functionality.

Summary

- There are two main Views in Live—Session View and Arrangement View—and you can use [tab] to switch between them.
- Most of the various areas of the Live interface can be shown, hidden, and resized as needed.
- The question mark key [?] shows Info View, which will give contextual help for any part of the program you place your mouse over.
- Live saves your work into a Project folder, which contains (among other things) your Live Sets.
- Live Sets contain the edits you make, but Sets do not contain any audio unto themselves. Instead, a Live Set merely references the audio files you choose.
- The Live Browser is your interface to accessing audio and MIDI files, Instruments, and Effects Devices.

Chapter 2

AUDIO CLIPS AND SESSION VIEW

O kay, you've got the basics taken care of. Let's make some music!

The primary building block of any Live Set is the Clip. Clips come in two flavors: Audio Clips and MIDI Clips. This chapter will deal with Audio Clips, and constructing a Set in Session View.

When you use a digital audio file in your Set, Live creates what is called a Clip out of it. A Clip is simply a wrapper for the audio content it contains that allows for a wide assortment of playback parameter assignments such as pitch, volume, Looping parameters, Warp Markers, Launch Modes, and Clip Envelopes. These are some of the primary functions that make Live the powerful sound-sculpting tool that it is.

There are four kinds of Tracks in Live: Audio Tracks, MIDI Tracks, Return Tracks, and the Master Track. We will explore each of these eventually, beginning with Audio Tracks. Audio Tracks can record and play back Audio Clips. An Audio Track in Live is a lot like a channel on a hardware audio mixer: a Track takes in an audio signal; allows you to change the signal's volume, panning, EQ, and effects settings; and then hands that signal on to the Master Track, where is it combined with other signals for output so you can hear these combined signals through your speakers or headphones.

When you first open Live, the program starts you off with two Tracks: an Audio Track called 1 Audio and a MIDI Track called 2 MIDI. In Session View, the vertical columns under the Track names are called Tracks. The gray boxes on these Tracks are called empty Clip Slots. This is where we will put (and later record) our Audio and MIDI Clip data.

Here are a few things you should know about Audio Clips and Audio Tracks:

· An Audio Clip plays on an Audio Track.
· An Audio Track can play back only one Audio Clip at a time.
· An Audio Clip can be either mono (one channel) or stereo (two channels).
· An Audio Track can have both mono and/or stereo Audio Clips on it at the same time.

Let's see Audio Clips in action:

Exercise 2.1—Audio Tracks and Clips in Session View

For this exercise—and most of the exercises—you will need the content folder that came with your book.

2.1.1—Importing and Launching Your First Clip

Do It! Here are two ways to set up your Exercise 2.1 Project:

- You can continue from right where you left off at the end of Exercise 1 and use File > Save As... to save the Set as My Exercise 2.1.als, or
- Open the supplied Exercise 2.1.als from the Book Content > Exercise Sets folder. It is exactly the same as a new Set. Save it as My Exercise 2.1.

Ready?

1. Make sure the Browser is visible:
- Click on the Show/Hide Browser triangle in the upper-left corner of the screen.
- Press [cmd-opt-b/ctrl-alt-b] until it is visible.
2. Click on the first of the three File Browser icons in the Browser.
3. Navigate to Book Content > Sounds to Sample > Drum Loops.

This is the folder of downloaded content provided with your book that you saved to your hard drive.

4. Find the file called MT_Beats_125_07.wav and click on it once.

A small waveform appears at the bottom of the Browser in the Preview tab showing you a visual representation of the audio. To the left of the waveform is a button with a pair of headphones on it. Click on this to preview the file. Alternately, you can use [shift-return] or [right arrow] to preview a highlighted Track in the Browser.

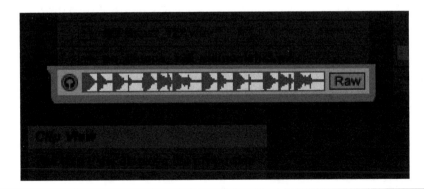

Pic. 2a: The Preview tab and Preview button in the Browser.

5. Click-and-drag this Clip onto the top Clip Slot on the Track named 1 Audio.
   Your Audio Track should now look something like this:

Pic. 2b: The Audio Clip MT_Beats_125_07.wav on the Audio Track 1 Audio.

You now have an Audio Clip on your Audio Track! Live assigns a random color to the new Audio Clip in the Session View Clip grid. Note the new Clip View box that comes up at the bottom of your screen when you add a new Clip. For now, leave this alone. We'll get into that shortly.

6. On the left-hand side of the MT_Beats_125_07 Clip in the Clip grid, you will see a triangle pointing to the right. This is the Clip Launch button. Click on it. You should hear your Clip play.

Notice that the Clip Loops automatically. In the Track Status Display just below the Clip grid, you'll see a number, a small and animated pie chart, and another number.

Pic. 2c: The Track Status Display area just below the Clip grid.

- The first number shows the number of times the Loop has played.
- The small pie chart is a visual representation of the percentage of the Loop that has played so far.
- The final number is the number of quarter-note beats in the current Clip.

You may be wondering, "How do I stop the Clip?" There are several different ways to stop a Clip that is playing, each of which does something slightly different. Try them all:

- Click on any of the Clip Stop buttons (the squares) in any of the empty Clip Slots on the same Track.
- Click on the Clip Stop button in the Track Status Display. This does the same thing as clicking on an empty Clip Slot's Stop button, but sometimes all the Clip Slots are full of Clips, so this provides a Clip Stop button that is always visible.
- Click on the Stop All Clips button on the Master Track all the way to the right. This will stop all Clips on all Tracks, but leaves global playback of the Set still running. You'll discover why this is useful later.

Pic. 2d: The Stop All Clips button on the Master Track.

- Click on the Stop button in the Control Bar at the top-middle of the interface, or press [spacebar]. This stops playback of the entire Set.

2.1.2—Adding a Second Clip

Before moving on, let's get rid of the 2 MIDI Track. We won't be using it for this exercise.

7. Click on the Track name to highlight it, and the press the [delete] key on your keyboard, or go Edit > Delete.

Do It! Let's add our second Clip while the first one is playing!

8. Click on the Launch button on the MT_Beats Clip you added previously to Track 1 Audio so that it plays.
9. With the first Clip still playing, in the Browser, return to the same folder as before (Book Content > Sounds to Sample > Drum Loops). Click on another Loop in the same folder.

If the Preview button is still lit blue at the bottom of the Browser, you should now hear the new file you selected playing in sync with the MT_Beats Clip. Very cool! This is made possible by Live's Warping engine and it is part of the magic of Live! Scroll through the list, single-clicking on each file one at a time or using the Up/Down Arrow keys, previewing each of these Loops with your first Loop. Some will sound good together, while others not so much.

Important! How a file plays back when previewed in the Browser depends on whether Live is currently playing:

- If Live is currently stopped (the Play button is black in the Control Bar area) and you click on a file in the Browser, Live will play back that Clip at its original tempo.
- If Live is already playing (the Play button is green in the Control Bar) and you click on a file in the Browser, Live will attempt to play back the file at the Set's master tempo, in sync with your other Clips.
- If Live is already playing and you want to preview a Clip at its original tempo and not in sync with the Set's master tempo, click on the Raw button to the right of the preview waveform at the bottom of the Browser window. This may be useful for Clips without a lot of rhythmic content, such as atmospheric backgrounds, sound effects, or spoken-word Clips to name a few.

Okay, let's continue:

10. Preview the file s2s_tt_lighttribal_125_lawn3.wav. These two sound pretty good together.
11. Rather than dragging the file over to a Clip Slot, this time do one of the following:
- Double-click on the file name.
- Highlight the file and press [return].

Either of these actions will create a new Track and put the selected file into the top Clip Slot on the new Track, here called 2 Audio.

12. The new Clip on the new Track is currently not playing. Launch s2s_tt_lighttribal_125_lawn3 with its Launch button. The Launch button may flash for a moment or two, and then when the beat comes around again, the Clip launches in sync with the first Clip.

Important! You may notice that the level meter on the Master Track turns red intermittently. This means that the combined volume of all your Tracks has exceeded the total available dynamic range, and has gone into "clipping," which is harsh, digital distortion. You can always correct this in one of three ways:

- Lower the Master Volume slider until the Master level meter turns green again.
- Lower the Track Volume slider on your individual Tracks until the Master level meter turns green again.
- Lower the Clip Gain of individual Clips.

Each of these accomplishes the task, but each will impact future volume-related decisions as well. For now,

13. Lower the Master Volume slider to −10 dB. You can see the exact level as you move the slider in the Status Bar at the bottom of Live's interface.

You may need to increase your speaker's volume slightly to compensate for the drop in level.

Pic. 2e: Two Track Volume sliders, Two Return Track Volume sliders, and the Master Volume slider.

2.1.3—Set Tempo and the Global Quantize Value

Important! The synchronization of these two Clips is made possible by two very important controls at the top of your screen:

• The first control is far to the left in the Tempo box where you see the number 120, which stands for 120 beats per minute (bpm). The Tempo value sets the tempo for the entire Set, and when new Clips are added to the Set, Live will attempt to play the Clip back at this tempo, in sync with all of the Set's other Clips.

Pic. 2f: The Global Tempo box in the Control Bar.

• The second control is in the middle at the top, where it says 1 Bar. This is the Global Quantization value. When you attempt to launch a new Clip during playback, Live will wait until the next Global Quantization value to start playback of the Clip. At the current setting of 1 Bar, Live will wait until the next bar after you click on the Launch button to actually play the Clip. Depending on when you click on the Launch button, this could be almost instantaneously, or several beats later.

Pic. 2g: The Global Quantization value in the Control Bar.

Do It! Let's test these two concepts:

14. With either or both of the Clips playing, click-and-drag in the Tempo box and hear the tempo change. Try going to the far extremes (20, then 999) to hear your Clips do some crazy things. When done, return the tempo to 120 bpm.
15. Launch one Clip, either will do.
16. Change the Global Quantization value to 4 Bars.
17. Now click on the Launch button of the second Clip.

The Launch button flashes until the next bar number divisible by four comes around, such as 4, 8, 12, or 100.

18. Stop the second Clip.
19. Change the Global Quantization value to 1/4.
20. Play the second Clip.

It will start at the next quarter note now, which is much more often, and can make for some very interesting syncopated rhythms!

21. When you are done experimenting with this, set the Global Quantization value back to 1 Bar.
22. Stop playback. The [spacebar] is your friend.

We will return again and again to these two concepts. They are foundational to what makes Live such a unique program.

2.1.4—A Third Clip and Launching Scenes

Do It! This groove needs some bass! Let's add our third Clip and then explore the concept of Scenes:

23. In the Browser, head over to Book Content > Sounds to Sample > Bass. Audition some bass lines. Double-click on the file MT_Bass_125_A_04.wav to send it to its own new Audio Track—in this case, 3 Audio.
24. Click on the Stop All Clips button in the lower-right corner of the grid.

This will stop any previously playing Clips.

Notice that if you press [spacebar] to start playback after clicking on Stop Clips, nothing plays. Even though the global bars and beats indicator is incrementing in the Control Bar, none of the Clips have been launched since you pressed Stop Clips.

Look all the way to the right in the Clips grid to the Track called Master. Notice that instead of empty Clip Slots, this Track has numbers and Launch buttons already. These are known as Scenes.

25. Click on the Launch button next to the Master cell marked 1.

All three Clips on all three Tracks begin to play! You have just launched your first Scene.

A Scene is simply an elegant way to launch an entire horizontal row of Clips across all the Tracks at once. As you are about to see, Scenes also give you an easy way to experiment with groupings of Clips and to create some arrangement possibilities.

26. Select your very first Clip, MT_Beats, by clicking once on the Clip's name (not the Launch button).

Now duplicate it by doing one of the following:

· Press [cmd-d/ctrl-d].
· Go Edit > Duplicate.
· [Ctrl-click/right-click] on the Clip to bring up a contextual menu and choose Duplicate.

You can do this on multiple Clips at once as well:

27. Make a multiselection of all three Clips in the first Scene across all three Tracks by doing one of the following:
- Click-and-drag a box around the three Clips in Scene 1.
- [Cmd-click/ctrl-click] on the three Clips in Scene 1 one at a time.
- Click once on the MT_Beats Clip, hold down Shift, and [shift-click] on the MT_Bass_125_A_04 Clip.
28. Press [cmd-d/ctrl-d] twice to duplicate the selected row of Clips twice. You should now have three rows of all three Clips.

Pic. 2h: Three Scenes of three Clips on three Tracks.

This action can be performed on Scenes as well, but for now, do not duplicate any Scenes.

How is this useful, you ask? Time to chisel at the marble and reveal the statue within! You can get rid of Clips as easily as you duplicate them:

29. Select the first Clip on 2 Audio and do one of the following:
- Press the [delete] key.
- Go Edit > Delete.
- [Ctrl-click/right-click] on the Clip and choose Delete from the contextual menu.
30. Also delete the first and second Clips on the 3 Audio Track. Your Clip grid should now look like this:

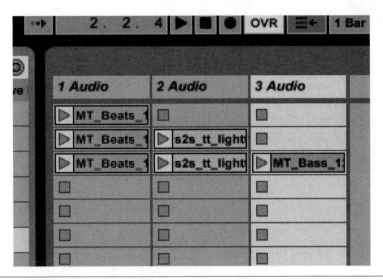

Pic. 2i: Three different Scene variations of three Clips.

Here is an alternate way that I like to use to launch Scenes:

31. Click on the name of the first Scene (not the Launch button) on the Master Track to highlight the Scene. The Scene Slot turns yellow, and the rest of the Scene is highlighted white.
32. Press the [enter] key. The first Scene launches, and the second Scene is now highlighted.
33. After the Scene has played for a few bars, hit [enter] again. The second Scene is launched, and now the third Scene is highlighted.
34. Launch the third Scene in the same way when you are ready.
    Want to play a previous Scene? No problem:
35. Use the [up/down arrow] keys to highlight the desired Scene, and then press [enter] to launch it.

Cool! With minimal keystrokes you can step through your Scenes at any pace you like. No need for precision mouse clicking! Sometimes aiming and timing a mouse-click on those small Launch buttons can be tricky. Using [up/down arrows] and [enter] offers a much easier and more reliable method. You can also configure a MIDI controller to do the same thing, and then you won't need the keyboard or the mouse!

As you step through these three Scenes, notice these three simple Clip combinations. As you can hear and see, we have the beginnings of a simple arrangement emerging.

Note that you can play the Scenes in any order you like, remixing your basic arrangement on the fly. Since each of these Scenes currently Loops indefinitely, we have not yet had to commit to determining how long each of these Scenes will ultimately play. Instead we have simply identified that these Clip combinations work well together and might be used in these groupings in our final arrangement. You could make Scenes for different verses, a chorus, a bridge, an intro, and a finale. Ultimately, I will show you how to turn your Session View Clips and Scenes into an arrangement in Arrangement View. For now, let's explore Audio Clips a bit more.

2.1.5—Renaming Scenes, Tracks, and Clips

It is a great idea to get in the habit of renaming things as you go along so that you can quickly identify the elements of your Set. In Live, this is very simple: highlight the object you would like to rename and do one of the following:

- Press [cmd-r/ctrl-r].
- Go Edit > Rename.
- [Ctrl-click/right-click] on the item and choose Rename from the contextual menu.

Do It! Do the following to rename your three Tracks:

36. Click on the Track name 1 Audio. Use one of the three previous methods to rename it to Beats.
37. Instead of pressing [return] to commit your renaming, instead press [tab], which jumps you to the next Track and highlights the name of 2 Audio for renaming. Much easier! Rename 2 Audio as Perc.
38. Press [tab] again, and rename 3 Audio as Bass.
39. Click in the first Scene on the Master Track currently named 1, and rename it as Intro. Press [tab]. Rename the second Scene as Add Perc. Press [tab] again and rename the third Scene as Add Bass.
40. Rename the Beats Track's Clips as MT_Beats, the Perc Track's Clips as Lighttribal, and the Bass Track's Clip as MT_Bass.

Important! Renaming a Clip does not rename the file on your hard drive. Don't forget!

41. Save your Set by pressing [cmd-s/ctrl-s].

Exercise 2.2—Clip View Properties

When you click on a Clip's colored box (not the Launch button), Live displays the Clip's Clip View properties in the Detail View at the bottom of the interface. The Clip View boxes contain many variables and concepts worth exploring.

At the bottom left of the Clip View area you will notice three little yellow buttons: one is the letter L, one is a small image of a waveform, and one is the letter E. Each of these buttons shows and hides a box of the Clip View:

- The Clip box is always shown and cannot be hidden.
- The L button shows and hides the Launch box.
- The waveform squiggle button shows and hides the Sample box.
- The E button shows and hides the Envelopes box.

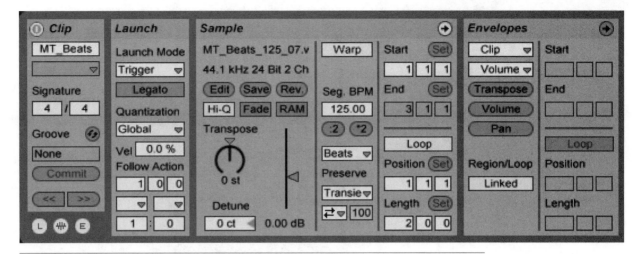

Pic. 2j: The Clip View boxes and their Show/Hide buttons.

Go ahead and turn all three buttons on if any of them are off. We will go through each of them.

To the right of these four boxes is the Sample Display. Here you can view a Clip's progress as it plays back and make other adjustments depending on whether the Sample or Envelopes box is currently active. You can toggle between which box is active by clicking on either the Sample or the Envelopes box's title bar.

Here is what each of these Clip View boxes does in a general sense:

- Clip—The Clip box is for activating/deactivating, renaming, changing the color, changing the time signature, or changing the applied Groove of the current Clip.
- Launch—The Launch box controls how the Clip responds to Launch commands, and what it does after it has been launched.
- Sample—The Sample box controls Clip gain, tuning, Warping and Warp Mode, and start, end, and Looping values.
- Envelope—The Envelopes box is where you apply Clip Envelopes, allowing you to automate (vary over time) just about any parameter associated with the Clip.

The following exercises will walk you through several of the Clip View's key features.

2.2.1—Clip Gain (volume)

Do It! Get ready to learn about Clip View. There are two ways to get started:

- You can continue from right where you left off at the end of Exercise 2.1 and use File > Save As… to save the Set as My Exercise 2.2.als, or
- You can open Exercise 2.2.als from the supplied Sets in Book Content > Exercise Sets, and then perform a Save As... and save your Set as My Exercise 2.2.als.

The relative volume level of the Lighttribal Clip on the Perc Track seems a little high to my ears. While you could lower the Track volume in the mixer, that would also lower the volume of future Clips that you may want to put on this Track. Instead, lower the Clip's gain, which you can think of as another word for "volume."

1. Click on the first instance of the Lighttribal percussion Clip in Clip Slot 2 on the Perc Track. The Clip's properties come up in the Detail View at the bottom of your screen.

2. Make sure that the Sample box is visible (which it should be already) by enabling the squiggly waveform radio button at the bottom-left corner of the Detail View.

In the Sample box, note the vertical slider with 0.00 dB appearing below it. This is your Clip Gain slider.

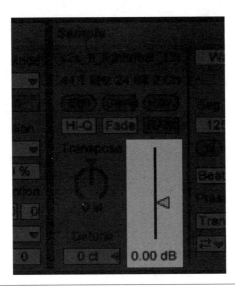

Pic. 2k: The Clip Gain slider.

3. Lower this Clip's gain (volume) to −8.09 dB by doing one of the following:
-   Click on the triangle and pull it downward.
-   Click anywhere on the Clip Gain slider and use your computer keyboard's [up/down arrow] keys to adjust it.
-   Click on the 0.00 dB value at the bottom: a box appears around it, and you can now type in any value you like.

Doing this means that every time this Clip is played back, it will play back at a little more than eight decibels less than it was recorded at.

4. Now click on the duplicate of Lighttribal just below this Clip in Clip Slot 3 of the Clip grid. Notice that the volume of this Clip still reads as 0.00 dB.

Important! Clip Gain and all other Clip parameters are specific to that Clip only! Adjusting one Clip will not adjust the parameters of its duplicates. Every Clip in the grid can have radically different Clip View properties, even though they all reference the same original audio file. This is an awesomely powerful feature of Live, as you will see!

If you want the Gains of both of these Clips to be the same, you can accomplish this in one of several ways:

-   Manually lower each of the individual Clip Gains one at a time.
-   Change the Gain of the first Clip and duplicate that Clip again, overwriting your previous Clip.
-   Multiselect all of the Clips whose Gain you wish to change and change them simultaneously.

At different times, each of these techniques will be the way to go depending on what needs doing. Let's try each of these:

5. Since you have already changed the first of the two Lighttribal Clip's Gain, let's just duplicate it over the second Clip: Highlight the first Clip (whose Clip Gain you already changed to read –8.09 dB) and hit [cmd-d/ctrl-d] to duplicate the Clip down to the next Slot. Although it does not look as though anything has happened, since there was already a Clip in the third Slot, the third Clip Slot is now an exact copy of the second Clip Slot, including the Gain change you made. Confirm this by clicking on the Clip in the third Slot: its Clip Gain should now also read –8.09 dB.

6. Click on the first MT_Beats Clip in Clip Slot 1 on the Beats Track. Hold down [shift] and click on the third (and last) Clip in Slot 3 to multiselect all three duplicate Clips. When you do so, the Clip View changes to something like this:

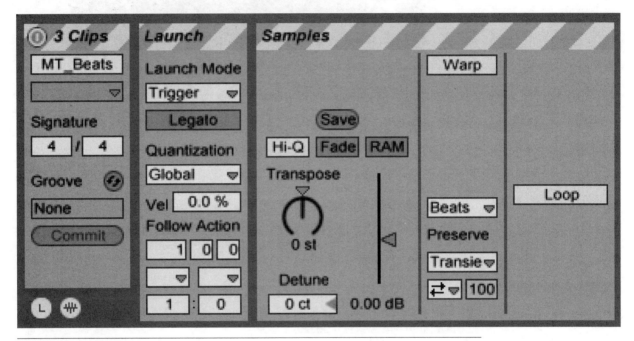

Pic. 2l: Multiselected Clips.

The "candy cane" diagonal stripes are there to indicate that you have selected multiple Clips and are potentially about to adjust the parameters for multiple Clips simultaneously.

7. With all three MT_Beats Clips still multiselected, bring the Clip Gain slider down just slightly to –2.31 dB. All three Clips' Gain values have been adjusted.

8. Select MT_Bass Clip on the Bass Track so you can see its properties in the Detail View area. Click on the Gain value of 0.00 dB, type in "–3", and press [return]. The volumes are a bit more balanced now.

2.2.2—Clip Transposition

Do It! Let's change a new parameter: Clip Transpose. Tuning elements—even drums—so that they work together is essential for making a harmonious mix:

9. Launch your third Scene, Add Bass, so that all three Clips are playing.

10. Select your MT_Bass Clip on the Bass Track by clicking on its name, which will bring up Clip View for that Clip.

11. Click-and-drag the Transpose dial and listen to the pitch of your bass line change in semitone (st) steps. As you go beyond a few semitones in either direction, you will hear the tone of the sound change more and more dramatically.

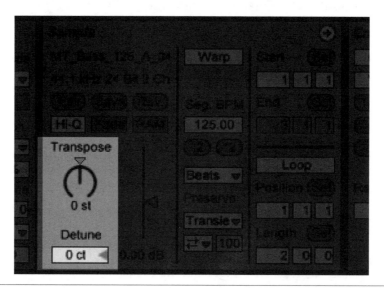

Pic. 2m: The Transpose dial and Detune box.

12. While you are at it, go ahead and click-and-drag in the Detune box as well. This is a subtler pitch adjustment using cents (ct). There are 100 cents in a semitone, so the Detune adjustment could be used for fine-tuning a performance that might be less than a semitone out of pitch with your Set. Note that you can adjust this value indefinitely in either direction, and the value will "wrap around," working in tandem with the Transpose value. Once you go upward in pitch past 50 cents (ct) (the value, not the rapper!) in the Detune box, you will notice that the Transpose value increments by 1 and the Detune value becomes –49 ct. The same is true when rolling the Detune value downward.

13. Reset the Transpose and Detune to 0.

The Transpose and Detune values work closely with the Warp Mode settings (described in chapter 3, "Warping, Quantizing, and Grooves") and with the Transpose Envelope described later in this chapter.

2.2.3—Looping and Nonlooping Clips
Thus far we have worked exclusively with Clips that repeat, or Loop, as well as with Clips that are Warped to fit the tempo of our Set. Let's explore what these controls are for, and find a few instances in which these controls are not necessarily desirable.

14. In the Browser, head on over to Book Content > Sounds to Sample > Atmospheric and preview a file called TEMFX01-Atmospheric11.wav. Spooky and delicious! Drag this file into the big open gray area in the Clip grid that is labeled Drop Files and Devices Here, and do what it tells you to do: drop it there! Live creates a new Audio Track and puts this Clip in the first Clip Slot, parallel with your first instance of MT_Beats, in the Scene you labeled as Intro.

15. Rename this new Track—currently named 4 Audio—as One Shots, and rename the new Clip as Atmospheric.

16. This Clip, being as long as it is, is not a Clip that you would necessarily want to hear over and over; hearing it once through as an introductory atmospheric mood setter should be enough. So, in the Clip View, on the Sample box, turn off Looping by deselecting the Loop button. Play the Intro Scene now, and listen to this Clip playing along with MT_Beats until the Atmospheric Clip completes. It will not Loop—it just ends, while MT_Beats continues. I call these nonlooping types of Clips (you guessed it) "one-shots."

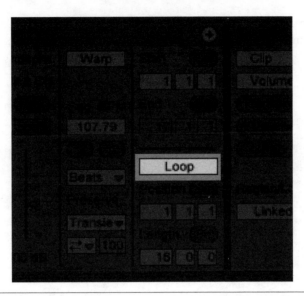

Pic. 2n: The enabled Loop button in Clip View.

At the same time, those two Clips by themselves get a little boring. Let's do something to add a little variation.

If you are playing the Intro Scene and you click on the Launch button for Scene 2, Add Perc, the Atmospheric Clip will stop playing because there is a Stop button in the second Clip Slot on your new One Shots Track. If you were to duplicate the Atmospheric Clip in Clip Slot 1 to this second Clip Slot, you would hear the Atmospheric Clip restart when you triggered the Add Perc Scene, and that is not very interesting, either. Instead, do this:

17. Click in the second (empty) Clip Slot on One Shots, below the Atmospheric Clip, and do one of the following:
• Press [cmd-e/ctrl-e].
• Go Edit > Remove Stop Button.
• [Ctrl-click/right-click] on the empty Clip Slot and choose Remove Stop Button from the contextual menu that appears.

This removes the Stop command from being triggered when this Scene is launched. If a Clip on this Track is already playing when you launch this Scene it will continue to play, since there is no longer a Clip Stop button to stop it.

18. Now, launch Scene 1, Intro, and let it play for a few measures. Once it has established itself, launch Scene 2, Add Perc.

The Atmospheric Clip continues to play while the Lighttribal Clip on the Perc Track is added. Nice! It adds a bit of interest while the Atmospheric Clip continues to evolve.

Now do something similar with a short Clip of a crash cymbal to punctuate the entrance of your Bass Clip in Scene 3.

19. Navigate to Book Content > Sounds to Sample > Crashes and drag the file The 80s. wav onto Clip Slot 3 of One Shots next to your MT_Bass Clip. Take the Clip Gain slider down to –8.09 dB. Turn Looping off for this Clip as well, so that it plays only once. (A Looping crash cymbal is a terrible thing! It sounds like a marching band, doesn't it? Ouch!)

20. Play through your first three Scenes, advancing when it feels right to do so. You needn't wait for the end of the Atmospheric Clip. When the time feels right, click on the Add Bass Scene and get your groove on with the bass line. It's starting to feel like a song now, right?

These are two examples of nonlooping Clips that can add variation to your Session View arrangement. Here is what your Clip grid should look like by now:

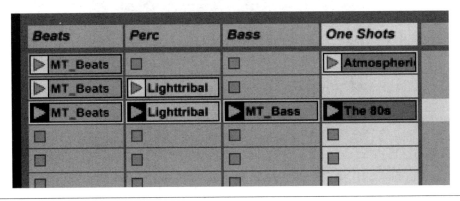

Pic. 2o: The Clip grid in progress.

2.2.4—Sample Editor Navigation Controls

Although we have worked with the Loop Brace to change the Loop Length, Loop Start, and Loop End values, we have not really needed to do any detailed editing in the Sample Editor thus far. Since that is about to change, let's take a moment to learn how to navigate the Sample Editor. For this section, let's use the Atmospheric Clip that we added previously.

21. Click on the Stop All Clips button on the Master Track.

22. In the Clip grid, click on the Atmospheric Clip's name in the first Clip Slot on the One Shots Track to bring up its Clip View properties.

Cool! If you want to make the Sample Editor larger so you can see more detail of the waveform, remember that you can click on and vertically drag the black divider between the Mixer and the Detail View area.

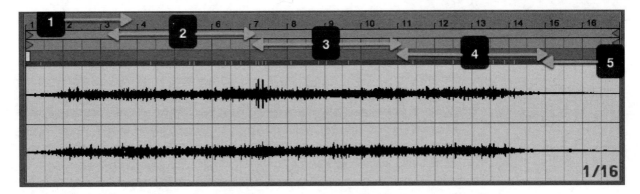

Pic. 2p: The Sample Editor Navigation Controls: Warp set to On.

Depending on whether a Clip's Warp button is enabled, the number and type of available controls in the Sample Editor will logically change. The more complex of these two states, and the one you may find yourself using most often, is when Warp is set to On (the way it presently is in this Clip), so let's look at these controls. The navigation controls in the Sample Editor with Warp set to Off represent a simplified version of these controls, as you will see.

Let's define some of the areas of the Sample Editor window when Warp is set to On:

- 1. Sample Display Timeline—The timeline shows the bar and beat divisions for the Clip. It is also used for navigation: as you mouse over the timeline, your cursor changes to a magnifying glass icon. Clicking-and-dragging on the timeline will zoom and scroll your view of the Clip's waveform.

- 2. The Loop Brace—As we previously saw, the Loop Brace is a visual representation of the Clip's Loop Start and End points. Clicking-and-dragging either end of the Loop Brace will adjust the Loop Start or End, respectively, and clicking-and-dragging in the middle of the Loop Brace will relocate the entire Loop, both Start and End simultaneously (provided that the Loop length has been shortened, creating room to move the Loop Brace either forward or backward in time).

- 3. Clip Start/End/Playback—The third area down from the top has triangle markers representing the Clip's Start and End values. These can be set independently from the Loop Start/End Brace above it. Mousing over the area between the Clip Start and End markers turns your cursor into a Speaker icon, and clicking there will launch the Clip from that point on the timeline. Note that the actual playback point and timing is governed by the current Global Quantization value, so that launching the Clip in this manner will still keep it in sync with your other Clips. Also note that mousing over the lower half of the waveform display will turn your cursor into a Speaker icon and clicking there will also launch the Clip from that point in a similar fashion.

- 4. The Warp Marker zone—The next area down concerns Warp Markers. Note the yellow Warp Marker at the start of this (or any Warped) Clip. Warp Markers are for manipulating a Clip's relationship to tempo, and are covered in chapter 3, "Warping, Quantizing, and Grooves." For now, do not click in this area.

- 5. Transient zone—This area just above the waveform works together with the Warp Marker zone above it. In essence, this thin strip indicates sudden jumps in the waveform's amplitude (volume) with little white marks, suggesting logical places to add a Warp Marker. Transients are also explored in chapter 3, "Warping, Quantizing, and Grooves."

Let's see some of these controls in action:

23. Launch the Atmospheric Clip by itself (not the whole Intro Scene). As the Clip plays, a vertical line shows the position of playback within the Clip, moving slowly across the waveform.

24. Roll your cursor anywhere over the timeline in the Sample Editor: it changes to a Magnifying Glass icon. Click with the magnifying glass and drag it downward a ways: The waveform magnifies, or "zooms in." (You can also use the [+] and [-] keys to zoom horizontally.)

25. Before releasing the mouse button, drag left and right: The waveform scrolls left and right. (You can also use [left arrow] and [right arrow] to scroll the view horizontally.)

26. Would you like the Sample Editor view to follow the playback position? Easy: Click on the Follow button in the Control Bar or press [cmd-f/ctrl-f].

Pic. 2q: The Follow button in the Control Bar.

If you zoom or scroll the view at all, Follow is turned off and you must reenable it again. That is why knowing the keyboard shortcut for this feature is essential. Also, you can toggle between page-by-page or continuous scrolling in Live's Preferences on the Look/Feel page.

Important! In the lower-right corner of your screen, you will see a small duplicate waveform down below the main one. This is known as the Clip Overview. Its purpose is to provide you with an overview of your Clip's waveform when you are zoomed in on a portion of it. The black box that currently frames a portion of the waveform, which is known as the Zooming Hot Spot, indicates the segment that you are currently viewing in the Sample Editor.

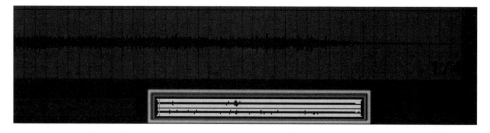

Pic. 2r: The Clip Overview area.

27. Use the magnifier on the timeline to continue to resize and scroll the Sample Editor View. Notice how the Zooming Hot Spot interacts with the Clip Overview31.

Important! The same navigational gestures you just learned for working with the timeline in the Sample Editor also work on the Clip Overview. You can jump the Zooming Hot Spot to any point in the timeline with a single click on the Clip Overview, and you can click-and-drag on the Zooming Hot Spot to zoom and scroll the view here as well. Try it!

28. Click on the Clip Overview to jump the Zooming Hot Spot to that location. Click-and-drag on the Zooming Hot Spot to zoom and scroll the Sample Editor window.

2.2.5—Alternate Loops

As I mentioned before, one audio file can be played back in an infinite number of ways using different Clip View settings for each duplicate. That is one of my favorite features of Live, for sure. Let's make some new variations of your primary three Clips to create a little buildup to the next section.

29. Multiselect the three left-most Clips in Scene 3, Add Bass: MT_Beats, Lighttribal, and MT_Bass. Press [cmd-d/ctrl-d] to duplicate these three Clips onto the fourth Scene.

Click on the new MT_Beats Clip you just made in the fourth Clip Slot. In the Clip View Sample box, find the Position and Length value boxes under the Loop toggle button. These control the start position and length of your Loop within the Clip. Currently, they are set to 1.1.1 and 2.0.0, respectively, which means "Start the Loop at (Position) bar 1, beat 1, sixteenth 1 (also known as the beginning of the Clip) and restart the Clip after playing for (Length) 2 bars, 0 beats, 0 sixteenth notes" (which happens to be the length of the entire Clip: 2 bars). In short, the entire Audio Clip is Looping every two bars. Let's change that.

Pic. 2s: The Loop Position and Length values in the Sample box.

30. Click in the middle Length box (currently 0), and then press the [down arrow] key until the Length reads 0.1.0, or one beat. Notice what happens in the Sample Editor to the right: The gray bar above the waveform (known as the Loop Brace) shortens to one beat and the rest of the sample is grayed out. If you launch this Clip right now, it will Loop only the first beat of this Clip.

31. Now change the Position values to 2.4.1, so that the last beat of the second bar of the Clip Loops. Notice what the Loop Brace is doing: it has moved over to the end of bar 2 and still covers only one beat. Launch it!

Let's move on to the newest Lighttribal Clip, to the right of the one you were just working on. This time let's use the Loop Brace to change the Length and Position values.

32. Put your cursor over the right end of the Loop Brace where the left-pointing triangle is. This is the Loop End indicator. Click-and-drag it to the left to 2.4.

33. Mouse over the left-most end of the Loop Brace: this is the Loop Start indicator. Drag it to 2.3. Notice that the Position value in the Sample box now reads 2.3.1 and the Length value reads 0.1.0. Play the Clip.

34. For a bit of variation, click-and-drag the Clip Start triangle (not the Loop Start triangle—the one just beneath that) all the way to the left to 1.1.1. Launch the Clip (or the Scene) and see the result of this.

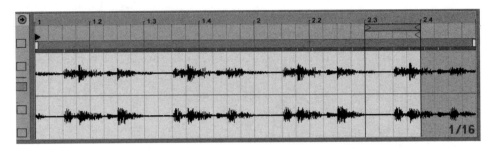

Pic. 2t: The Loop Brace, Loop Start, Loop End, and Clip Start indicators in the Sample Editor.

Cool! By moving the Clip Start away from the Loop Start you can have a Clip that plays from one point in the Clip and then Loops at a different place in the Clip. One common use of this is to have a series of Clips in a Scene that starts with a fill (perhaps a drum roll) and then moves into a repeating Loop without the fill. By putting it at the beginning of a series of Clips, you can choose when you want to transition into the Scene with the fill, but then Loop the rest of the Scene normally. There are lots of useful applications for this.

Finally, let's have a go with the bass Clip…

35. In the MT_Bass Clip in Scene 4, drag the Loop End indicator to 1.3 on the Sample Editor timeline, making the Clip Loop length two beats long, and starting at 1.1.1.

36. Launch the entire Scene 3, Add Bass, and then after a few bars launch into the Scene 4 you just made. A nice little buildup!

37. Let's rename this Scene and call it Buildup.

Although we have been making changes to some Clip View controls, up until this point we had not drastically altered any of these Clips, and they still retain a vast majority of the original file's feel and sound. But now that we have versions where we are looping a small segment, this seems like a reason to start renaming a few Clips. Let's rename the three Clips in the Buildup Scene.

38. Rename MT_Beats in the fourth Slot as MT_Beats Buildup 1.

39. Rename Lighttribal in the fourth Slot as Lighttribal Buildup 1.

40. Rename MT_Bass in the fourth Slot as MT_Bass Buildup 1.

Another thing I like to do to Clips that are different is to change their color so I remember that they are unlike the other Clips on the Track with the same name.

41. [Ctrl-click/right-click] on one of the Clips in the fourth Scene that you have just modified. See all the colorful boxes at the bottom of the contextual window? Pick one of these that is not the current color. Do this for all three Clips in the Buildup Scene.

I like to choose a color that is similar to the one it was before, so I can still associate it with the Clip it came from. If it was blue before, make this new version light blue. You will likely come up with your own ways of using Clip color to make sense of your Sets.

You may not be able to read the full titles of all your Clips at this point, as the Track is not wide enough. Let's expand the width of the Tracks so you can:

42. Put your cursor over the gray vertical divider between the Track names Beats and Perc. Your cursor changes to a bracket icon ( ]):

43. Click-and-drag this divider to the right to expand the width of the Beats Track. Repeat this for all the Tracks until you can read all the Clip names.

You can resize the Master Track and Return Tracks as well.

So you see, with a couple of simple variations of the Clip View properties, we have a very different-sounding Scene using the same three Clips.

2.2.6—Follow Actions

This is another unique feature of Live that I just adore. Follow Actions allow you to control (or randomize) how a series of sequential Clips on a Track relate to each other. You can create wonderful variations of Clips and then set their Follow Actions to determine what order to play them in. The following exercise will walk you through one of many possibilities.

Let's make Scene 5 return to the original Groove, and then add some new layers to explore Follow Actions.

44. Click on the Add Bass Scene name (not the Launch button) so the third cell down on the Master Track is highlighted. Then do one of the following:
- Press [cmd-c/ctrl-c] for Copy.
- Go Edit > Copy.
- [Ctrl-click/right-click] and select Copy from the contextual menu.
  You've now copied the Add Bass Scene to the Clipboard.

45. Click in the fifth Scene down (currently called 5) to highlight it, and do one of the following:
- Press [cmd-v/ctrl-v] for Paste.
- Go Edit > Paste.
- [Ctrl-click/right-click] and select Paste from the contextual menu.

46. You now have a fifth Scene. Rename it as Main Groove.
   All set. Now for three new Clips to use with Follow Actions:

47. Okay. Head over to Book Content > Sounds to Sample > Synth Loops, then find the file s2s_dt_synth_128_postwarvar1_Am.wav, and drag it onto a new Track in the fifth Scene Clip Slot next to your other new Clips in Main Groove. Rename it as Postwarvar1.

48. Drop s2s_dt_synth_128_postwarvar3_Am.wav in the Clip Slot just below the previous one, and then s2s_dt_synth_128_postwarvar4_Am.wav in the Clip Slot just below that. Rename them as Postwarvar3 and Postwarvar4, respectively.

49. Rename this new Track as Synth 1.

Your Clip grid should now look something like this:

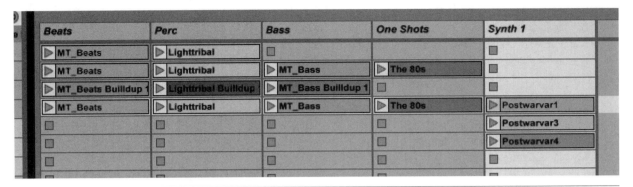

Beats	Perc	Bass	One Shots	Synth 1	
▷ MT_Beats	▷ Lighttribal	☐		☐	
▷ MT_Beats	▷ Lighttribal	▷ MT_Bass	▷ The 80s	☐	
▷ MT_Beats Buildup 1	▷ Lighttribal Buildup	▷ MT_Bass Buildup 1	☐	☐	
▷ MT_Beats	▷ Lighttribal	▷ MT_Bass	▷ The 80s	▷ Postwarvar1	
☐	☐	☐	☐	▷ Postwarvar3	
☐	☐	☐	☐	▷ Postwarvar4	
☐	☐	☐	☐	☐	
☐	☐	☐	☐		

Pic. 2u: The Clip grid in progress.

When you launch Scene 5, Main Groove, you will hear the first of the three new Clips play. Let's use Follow Actions so that all three will play in order and then Loop back to the start:

50. Click on Postwarvar1, the top-most Clip of the three. In the Clip View, on the Clip box, you will see the Follow Actions section:

Pic. 2v: The Follow Actions controls.

The three settings here are the following:

- Follow Action Time—This is the interval after which a Follow Action may occur.
- Follow Action A and B—Each of these two pull-downs represents a Follow Action that may occur at the Follow Action Time interval.
- Follow Action Chance A and B—These values express what the likelihood is that either Follow Action A or B will occur. If A is set to 5 and B is set to 1, there is a five to one likelihood that A will occur, and a one in five likelihood that B will occur. If either of these is set to 0 (the default), that action will never occur.

Yes, these controls are a little confusing at first glance, but stay with me! We will use them in a very straightforward way to get you started:

51. Set the Follow Action Time for this Clip to 4.0.0. Set the Follow Action A to Next. Set the Follow Action Chance A to 1.

This means that "after four bars, there is a one in one chance (or 100 percent) that the next Clip below will start playing." Easy enough? Try it! Play the Main Groove Scene and watch what happens: After all the Clips are triggered, the Clip below this one's (Postwarvar3) Launch button begins flashing right away, as if to say "I'm going to play next!" After four bars, it does just that. Let's keep going:

52. Click on the second Clip, Postwarvar3, and set the same settings for this Clip as the previous Clip.
53. Click on the final Clip, Postwarvar4. Notice that this Clip is only two bars long. Set the Follow Action Time for this Clip to 2.0.0. Set the Follow Action A to First. Set the Follow Action Chance A to 1. Play the Main Groove Scene to see what is happening.

Each of the three Clips plays in turn, and when the third one is done, it goes back to the first one and starts over. We've just created a 10-bar repeating phrase.

54. This new series of Clips seems a little loud compared with the rest. Since all three Clips are "equally too loud," using the Track Volume slider makes the most sense here. Grab the triangle on the Track Volume and bring it down to −1.0 dB (the exact level is shown in the Status Bar at the very bottom of your screen).

Pic. 2w: The Track Volume slider in the Mixer section.

55. Just for fun, go back to the Clip called The 80s in the fifth slot on the One Shots Track, and set this Clip to Loop every ten bars. This way, every time your Postwarvar Clip-phrase repeats, the crash cymbal will also sound.

Wow, we've done a lot so far. Congrats! Take a deep breath. Stretch. Grab a cup of tea, and come back: we've still got two more Audio Clip exercises to go, and I've saved the best two for last! Speaking of saving:

56. Save your Set: [cmd-s/ctrl-s].

Exercise 2.3—Clip Envelopes

So far in our growing Clip arrangement we have made some simple variations using volume, Looping, and Follow Actions. The next feature, Clip Envelopes, offers a simple way to vary Clip parameters over time, which opens up all kinds of new sonic possibilities. Although we will explore only the three most easily accessible Clip Envelopes to begin with, you can use Clip Envelopes to automate virtually any parameter you can think of.

Moreover, you can make an infinite number of different Clips from a single piece of audio or MIDI, allowing for incredible variety and flexibility. The specific settings that you select in each Clip are saved and stored in your Set and can be saved to the Live Library for future use in other Sets.

2.3.1—The Volume Clip Envelope, Draw Modes, and Grid Values

Do It! Let's get ready to work with Clip Envelopes. Here are two ways to get started:

- You can continue from right where we left off at the end of Exercise 2.2 and use File > Save As… to save the Set as My Exercise 2.3.als, or
- You can open Exercise 2.3.als from the supplied Sets in Book Content > Exercise Sets, and then perform a Save As... and save your Set as My Exercise 2.3.als.

Okay, now that you know how to navigate in the Sample Editor, let's grab a new Clip to work with:

1. Head over to the Book Content > Sounds to Sample > FX folder and double-click on the first file, CST 1.wav, to put it on its own new Track.
2. Move the Clip down to the fifth Clip Slot, which is on the Main Groove Scene.
3. Rename this Track as Synth 2. (No need to rename the Clip. It is already pretty simple and memorable.)
4. Play the Main Groove Scene to hear it in context.
5. If it is not already visible, click on the CST 1 Clip name in the Clip grid to ensure that the Clip's Clip View properties are visible in the Detail View at the bottom of your screen.

This CST 1 Clip is a little loud, and there is a raspy low note at the end of this phrase that doesn't sound great and conflicts with several other Clips' tonalities. You could use Clip Gain or Track Volume to fix the overall volume, but what about turning off that last note of the phrase? For that, you can use the Volume Clip Envelope.

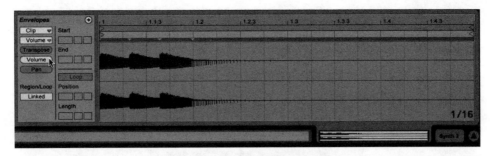

Pic. 2x: The Volume Clip Envelope button and the Sample Display overlaid with the Volume Clip Envelope.

6. In the Clip View area, click on the Volume button in the Envelopes box.

Important! The Sample Editor has two modes: Sample Display and the Envelope Editor. Thus far we have been working in Sample Display mode as we worked with the controls on that box. Notice the right-pointing arrows to the right of the Sample and Envelopes box names. The highlighted arrow indicates which Sample Editor mode you are currently in. Clicking on these arrows, or any control in either box, will switch you to the mode associated with that box. Easy.

When you click on the Volume button in the Envelopes box, the Sample Display area turns pink, as it is now overlaid with the Volume Clip Envelope and has switched to the Envelope Editor mode. Think of this pink area as a graph representing the Clip's relative volume level as it plays back.

In Envelope Editor mode, there are two Draw modes for modifying envelopes:

*   Draw mode On—In this mode, your cursor becomes a Pencil icon and you may draw in your envelopes by hand.
*   Draw mode Off—This mode is called Breakpoint Editing, and it is more like pinning down a rubber band to create smooth, gradual shifts from one breakpoint to another.

To toggle the Draw mode on and off, do one of the following:

*   Press [cmd-b/ctrl-b].
*   Click on the Draw mode switch (the one with the Pencil icon to the right of the Global Quantize value) at the top of your screen.
*   Go Options > Draw mode.

Pic. 2y: The Draw mode switch enabled.

For now, turn Draw mode on (make sure that the Pencil icon at the top of your screen is lit yellow, and your cursor turns into a pencil when it is over the Sample Display area).

7. Click and draw the Volume Envelope any way you like. Go crazy with it. Paint a landscape if you like. Hills and valleys. Play it back and hear the result.

Sounds pretty choppy, doesn't it? Look down in the lower right corner of the Sample Display/Envelope Editor. There's a fraction there, and yours likely says 1/16. (No, I'm not a mind reader—that is the default.) That is your Snap to Grid value. The envelopes you draw are currently snapping to a grid that is currently divided into 16th notes, hence the choppiness.

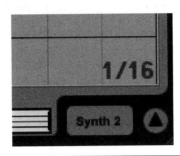

Pic. 2z: The current Sample Display grid value.

You can change the grid value in one of three ways:

· Pressing [cmd-1/ctrl-1] makes the grid value smaller, and pressing [cmd-2/ctrl-2] makes the grid value larger.
· Go Options > Narrow Grid or Options > Widen Grid.
· [Ctrl-click/right-click] and choose a grid value from the contextual menu.

What seems to fit our needs right now would be a 1/8T grid value, also known as eighth-note triplet divisions. To set the grid to 1/8T:

8. Press [cmd-2/ctrl-2] once to get to the 1/8-note grid value.
9. Press [cmd-3/ctrl-3] once to turn triplets on. (The other two methods described above have equivalents here as well: Options > Triplet Grid, or [ctrl-click/right-click] and choose Triplet Grid.) The grid value now reads 1/8T.
10. Using the Pencil icon, click anywhere on the waveform: the Volume Clip Envelope jumps to meet your Pencil. The 1/8T grid division is (conveniently) the length of one note. Click-and-drag the envelope to about 80% for the first three 1/8T divisions, which are the notes that we want to be slightly quieter. Those first three high notes are a little more bearable.
11. Now draw all the remaining quarter-note divisions down to 0% so that they will not sound at all. This gets rid of the buzzy low note altogether.

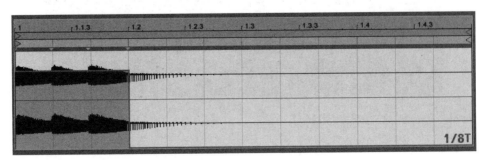

Pic. 2za: The final Volume Clip Envelope for CST 1: Draw mode is on, Snap to Grid is on.

You can use the Volume Clip Envelope to do some wonderful things such as stuttering a Clip on and off rapidly, creating a long fade-in, or randomizing the volume entirely.

One question you might be asking yourself at this point is, "Why do the units for measuring the volume envelope use a percentage as the scale? Wouldn't decibels be a better unit of measurement here?" I'm glad you asked! I, too, asked this question when I first used Clip Envelopes. But I soon realized why Ableton did it that way:

Important! Many Clip Envelope graphs are expressed as a percentage of the Clip's current value. In the case of Clip Volume, the red line at the top represents "100% of the current Clip Gain," and dragging the red line below 100% are percentages of the current Clip Gain value. This way you can still change the Clip Gain slider, and whatever pattern you have drawn here will be a relative amount (and therefore a percentage) of the Clip Gain value.

Now it makes sense!

2.3.2—The Pan Clip Envelope with Draw Mode Is On and Snap to Grid Is Off

Do It! Let's give this CST 1 Clip some motion. It's a little dead in the water:

12. Leave Draw mode on, or turn it on if it is not.
13. Do one of the following to toggle Snap to Grid to off:
- Press [cmd-4/ctrl-4].
- Choose Options > Snap to Grid (unchecked).
- Press [Ctrl-click/right-click] and choose Fixed Grid: Off.
14. Now use the Pencil icon to draw a Pan Clip Envelope that is completely free of constraint by the grid.

Nature is full of curves. You can make less mechanical-sounding curves this way. I went with something like this:

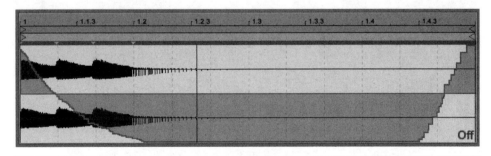

Pic. 2zb: The final hand-drawn curve for the Pan Clip Envelope: Draw mode is on, Snap to Grid is off.

Important! You may have noticed that the Pan adjustment here is also measured in percentages, just like Volume Clip Envelopes. Pan Clip Envelopes are also a relative adjustment, this time relative to the Track's Pan value in the Mixer. Change the value in the Mixer, and the Pan Clip Envelope will still adjust the Pan position relative to the new value.

2.3.3—The Transpose Clip Envelope and Breakpoint Editing

The third and final quick-chooser button we have not explored in the Envelopes box is the craziest: The Transpose Clip Envelope. Click on it, and get ready to party.

What you are looking at looks and functions a lot like the Pan Clip Envelope.

15. Go ahead and modify the Transposition Clip Envelope using one of the two methods you did previously.

    Now try one more:

16. Click on the Transpose Clip Envelope button.

17. Press [cmd-b/ctrl-b] to turn the Draw mode to Off.

    The Pencil icon at the top of your screen is now disabled.

18. Put your mouse over the red line that runs down the middle of the Sample Display area, and the line turns blue. (This just means that you are directly over the line.) Click-and-drag the (now) blue line while playing the Clip. This line controls the Transpose value, currently for the entire Clip in one big, long line.

19. Now double-click on the line. You've made what is called a "breakpoint."

20. Make another breakpoint somewhere else on the line. Now click-and-drag this second breakpoint somewhere. You are breakpoint editing. Hoorah!

    To remove a breakpoint, do one of the following:

- Double-click on it.
- Drag a selection across one or more breakpoints and press [delete].
- Drag a selection across one or more breakpoints and go Edit > Delete.

Experiment with this all you like with Transpose Clip Envelope breakpoints. Here's what I did. I kept it simple: The pitch slides from the first breakpoint at +2 st down to –19 st at the end of the third note at 1.2.

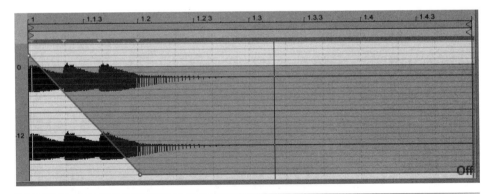

Pic. 2zc: The final Transpose Clip Envelope for CST1: Draw mode is off, Snap to Grid is off.

Cool! If you want to move between semitone values with your breakpoints, hold down [cmd/ctrl] while you drag a point. This is useful for making small pitch adjustments such as correcting an out-of-tune vocal phrase.

2.3.4—Unlinked Clip Envelopes, Looping and Nonlooping

In the previous three examples, all of the Clip Envelopes have been exactly as long as the Clip that you were working with. This doesn't have to be the case. Let's make two examples in which the Clip Envelope and actual Clip audio are unlinked from each other.

The first is going to be a short, Looping envelope over a longer, nonlooping Audio Clip to create a stutter effect:

21. Remember your Atmospheric Clip from the Nonlooping Clips exercise? One Shots Track, Clip Slot 1? Yes that one. Click on it to bring up its Clip View, and click on the Volume Clip Envelope button.

22. Under Region/Loop in the Envelopes box, toggle the Linked button so that it turns orange and reads Unlinked. Now the Clip and the Clip Envelope can be different lengths.

Pic. 2zd: The Linked Envelope button toggled to Unlinked.

23. Under the Loop button, set the length to 0.0.1, which is a 16th note in length. You now have a Volume Clip Envelope that is a 16th note in length, and it Loops.

24. Set your grid value to 1/32. ([Cmd-1/ctrl-1] and [cmd-2/ctrl-2] work well for adjusting grid value size.)

25. Make sure that Draw mode is turned on, and turn the volume off for the second 32nd note. Play the Intro Scene again. The Atmospheric Clip pulses on and off once every 16th note. This continues for the length of the Audio Clip. A bit more interesting, I think.

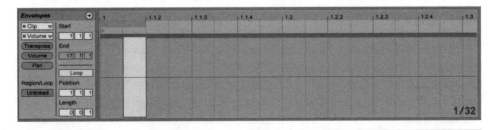

Pic. 2ze: A Looping, stuttering Volume Clip Envelope.

Another combination is a long, nonlooping Clip Envelope over a short, Looping Audio Clip. Here we go:

26. Remember the shortened version of the MT_Bass Clip you made for the Buildup Scene? It is on the Bass Track, and it's in the fourth Clip Slot down. You even changed the Clip's color to signify its uniqueness. Bingo! Click on it.

27. Click on the Transpose button in the Envelopes box.
28. Toggle the Linked Envelope button to Unlinked.
29. This time, also toggle the Envelope Loop button to Off.
30. Just above the Loop button, set the Envelope End value to 6.1.1. Although the Clip Loop Length is a half bar long, the Clip Envelope is now six bars long.
31. Turn Draw mode off.
32. Make a slow, steadily increasing Transpose Clip Envelope that starts at 0 ct at bar 1 and reaches 24 ct by bar 6. That looks like this:

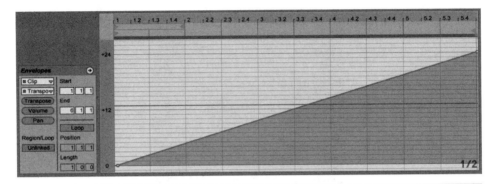

Pic. 2zf: An unlinked, nonlooping, steadily increasing Transpose Clip Envelope across six bars.

Play it back. The bass's pitch continues to rise across six bars of the envelope. Granted, it sounds a little cheesy right now, but we'll fix that with Warp Modes and effects soon enough.

33. Save your Set by pressing [cmd-s/ctrl-s].

Summary

- When you open a digital audio file in Live, Live makes an Audio Clip.
- An Audio Clip plays on an Audio Track, which can play back only one Audio Clip at a time.
- An Audio Clip can be either mono (one channel) or stereo (two channels), and an Audio Track can have mono and/or stereo Audio Clips on it at the same time.
- In Session View, Audio Clips are stored vertically in Clip Slots on an Audio Track, and can be played by clicking on their Clip Launch button.
- Clips can be stopped by clicking on an empty Clip Slot's Clip Stop button, the Track's Clip Stop button, the Master Track's Stop All Clips button, or by pressing the [spacebar], which stops Live's transport entirely.
- Audio files can be previewed in the Browser, either at the current Set's tempo or at their own original tempo, depending on whether Live is currently playing or not.
- Volume can be controlled at numerous places in Live: a Clip's Clip Gain slider, a Clip's Volume Envelope, a Track's Track Volume slider, and the Master Track's Master Volume slider. Each of these gain stages has a different effect on the gain stages after it.
- Warped Clips in a Live Set will play back at the Set's master tempo.
- Launching of a Set's Clips will be delayed to the next value set in the Global Quantization box.
- Clips aligned horizontally in the Clip grid are called "Scenes," and can be triggered simultaneously by clicking on that Scene's Scene Launch button.

- Many items in Live—such as a Track, Clip, or Scene—can be duplicated by pressing [cmd-d/ctrl-d] and deleted by pressing the [delete] key.

- Many items in Live—such as a Track, Clip, or Scene—can be renamed with the keyboard shortcut [cmd-r/ctrl-r].

- Many parameters that shape an Audio Clip's playback and sound can be found in that Clip's Clip View, which appears in the Detail View area when a Clip is clicked.

- The Clip View has four separate boxes, entitled Clip, Launch, Sample, and Envelope, respectively, the last three of which can be hidden and shown via their Show/Hide buttons.

- The Sample Display area is used for working with the Loop Brace, Start and End markers, or Clip Envelopes.

- Some Clip View properties can be changed on several Clips at once when multiple Clips are selected.

- You can change a Clip's pitch using the Transpose dial and Detune box.

- A Clip (or a portion of a Clip) can Loop, or not Loop. A nonlooping Clip is often referred to as a one-shot Clip.

- A Clip's color can be changed in the Clip panel in Clip View, or by [ctrl-clicking/right-clicking] on a Clip and selecting a new color.

- Follow Actions can control or randomize the order of playback of a series of vertically adjacent Clips.

- Clip Envelopes can control many parameters of how a Clip plays back. Volume, Pan, and Transpose Envelopes are three commonly used envelopes, and each of these has its own quick chooser button in the Envelopes box of Clip View.

- Clip Envelopes can be edited using either Draw mode or Breakpoint Envelope Editing mode. In either mode, Snap to Grid can be on or off.

- Envelopes may either be looping or nonlooping, and may be linked to the length of the Clip or unlinked and of any length.

Chapter 3

WARPING, QUANTIZING, AND GROOVES

Live's digital audio Warping engine is the key technology that makes a majority of the synchronization magic happen so seamlessly. It is what makes possible the ability to take multiple files of differing tempos and keys and use them together. All of the major DAW packages available today have some form of real-time digital audio time-stretching built in, but not only has Ableton been doing it for longer than most of them, in my opinion, they also do it better. Warping in Live is easier to use, and most importantly, sounds better at a wider range of stretching than any other tool I have used. As a result, this allows you to use a much wider array of sounds in your sessions.

Whether you realize it or not, you have already used the Warp engine in this Set quite a bit. Your three main Clips—MT_Beats, Lighttribal, and MT_Bass—were all created at 125 bpm, but the tempo of our Set is 120 bpm, and they all are playing in sync quite happily. Live's Warp engine "Warps" the 125 bpm Clips to fit the Set's tempo of 120 bpm. If you would like to hear what life would be like without Warping technology, go ahead and turn off the Warp button in the Sample box of one or more of your Clips in this Set, and play back the Scene that contains them. Have you ever listened to a DJ who can't seem to beat-match two Tracks together? It sounds like sneakers in a dryer, doesn't it? It's the same thing without Warping technology: total chaos!

But there is far more to Warping than just tempo alignment. Let's have a look.

Exercise 3.1—Warp Modes

3.1.1—The Clip View Warping and Tempo Controls

Do It! Let's prepare to work with Warping. Here are two ways to get started:

- You can continue from right where you left off at the end of Exercise 2.3 and use Save As... to save the Set as "My Exercise 3.1.als, or
- You can open Exercise 3.1.als from the supplied Sets in Book Content > Exercise Sets, and then perform a Save As... and save your Set as My Exercise 3.1.als.

The key to great- and creative-sounding Warping is in the Warp controls for each Clip, which can be found in the Sample box of each Clip's Clip View.

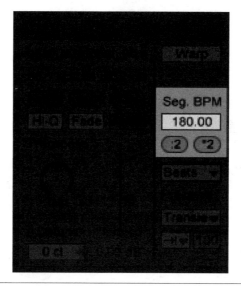

Pic. 3a: The Seg. bpm controls in Clip View.

This small box actually offers a very wide range of Warping possibilities, so let's take the time to get familiar with all that this area has to offer. To begin, we're going to add a new rhythm Clip for a breakdown section of our evolving Set:

1. Rename the eighth Scene in your Set as Breakdown1. It is currently named 8.
2. In the Browser, head over to Book Content > Sounds to Sample > Drum Loops. Find the file named Beat_reaktored_90.wav and click on it. You should hear it preview if the Preview "headphones" button is turned on.
3. Drag the sample Beat_reaktored_90.wav onto the eighth Clip Slot (the newly renamed Breakdown1 Scene) of your first Track, the Beats Track. This should leave a gap of two empty Clip Slots below the last instance of MT_Beats in Clip Slot 5. Rename the Clip as Beat_reaktored. Play the Clip by itself by playing the Breakdown1 Scene or clicking on the Beat_reaktored Clip's Launch button in the Clip grid. It now plays back quite a bit faster, at the Set's master tempo, 120 bpm.

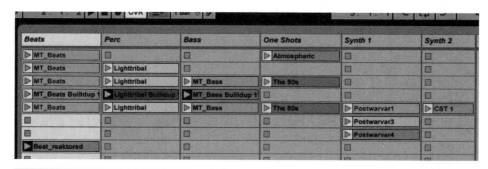

Pic. 3b: The Beat_reaktored Clip in the eighth slot on the Beats Track.

You may have noticed that many of the Clips you are working with have a number in their file name, such as the number 125 in s2s_tt_lighttribal_125_lawn3 or the number 90 in Beat_reaktored_90.wav. If you hadn't already guessed this, the number represents the original tempo at which the file was created, and this is the tempo at which the file will play back if you turn off the Warp button in Clip View. It is also the tempo you will hear if you click on the Clip in the Browser while Live's transport is stopped, or if you engage the Raw button.

4. While the Beat_reaktored Clip is playing, turn the Warp button on and off. The original tempo is quite a bit slower.

You will have to restart the Clip once it gets to the end, because the Warp and Loop functions are linked, and Loop will be turned off if Warp is disabled.

5. Before continuing, ensure that both the Warp and Loop buttons are engaged.

Playing back this 90 bpm Clip at the master tempo of 120 bpm sounds fine, but it is a little frenetic for a breakdown. What if you could hear this Clip playing at half speed instead?

Notice the box labeled Seg. BPM ("Segment BPM") currently shows a value of 90. This number represents Live's best guess at the Clip's original tempo. In this case, Live has guessed that the Clip's original tempo is 90 bpm, and speeds up the Clip to play it back at 120 bpm when the Warp button is engaged. But what would happen if we told Live that the Clip's original tempo was 180 bpm instead? Live would then slow down the Clip to play at 120 bpm. Let's try it:

6. Underneath the Seg. BPM box there are two buttons: one halves the original tempo, and the other doubles the original tempo. Click on the one to the right, marked *2. The Clip's original tempo now reads 180 and the Loop length now reads 4.0.0 rather than 2.0.0.
7. Play back the Clip using the Clip Launch button. It plays at half speed, which is equivalent to 60 bpm currently. Much better for a breakdown!
8. Just for fun, go ahead and hit the "halve the original tempo" (:2) button twice, so that the Seg. BPM reads 45. Play it back.

Yowza! One would need several more cups of coffee to appreciate a Clip playing that fast, which is effectively now 240 bpm. Click on *2 twice to put the Seg. Tempo back to 180 before someone goes into cardiac arrest!

9. To get a sense of how this is going to work with the rest of your Clips, remove the Stop button in the eighth Slot on the Synth 1 Track beneath the Postwarvar4 Clip (highlight the empty Clip Slot and press [cmd-e/ctrl-e]).
10. Now go back and launch the fifth Scene, named Main Groove, and let it play for a bar or two. Then click on the eighth Scene, Breakdown1. You should still hear the three Clips on Synth 1 playing in their Looping cycle while the Beat_reaktored Clip plays at half tempo on the Beats Track.

So the Seg. BPM box is key to letting Live know how fast or slow you want a Clip playing back relative to the Set's global tempo.

3.1.2—Warp Modes Overview

Now we are into the juicy stuff! Warp Modes allow you to try out one of several different time-stretching algorithms on a Clip. You can use these different algorithms to help the time-stretching sound more natural, or try out some more adventurous settings to create new and interesting variations of the Clip.

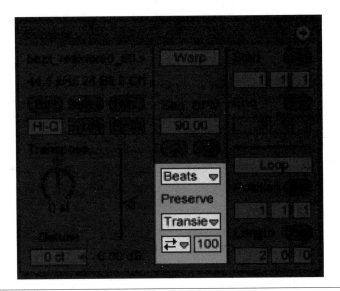

Pic. 3c: The Warp Mode controls in Clip View.

The default Warp Mode is called Beats, and that is what you will see in the Warp Mode pull-down menu, which you will find directly underneath the Halve/Double Original Tempo buttons. Open this pull-down menu and have a look at the other Warp Modes:

- Beats—This mode was created for rhythmic audio, and it is particularly good for drum Loops.
- Tones—This mode works well on audio with a clear sense of pitch.
- Texture—This mode is useful for complex and noisy sounds, such as multiple instruments playing together, a complex synth patch, or the sound of a bubbling brook.
- Re-Pitch—Re-Pitch works similarly to a record player in that pitch and playback speed are linked together: as the tempo slows the pitch decreases. The reverse is also true.
- Complex—This mode is devoted to working with a file of an entire mix, which often contains beat, tone, and texture information in the same Clip. The Complex algorithm uses as much as ten times the CPU load of the other modes, so watch your CPU load meter carefully when using this one.
- Complex Pro—As you might surmise, this mode is an extension of Complex mode, and uses even more complex computations and CPU resources. This mode works well with entire mixes whose pitch is also being transposed, and offers two parameters that Complex mode does not, for even more control over the sound.

Important! Managing your system's resources is a big and important part of making music on a computer. Learning about how your computer works and how to manage Live's resources is critical to using Live to its maximum potential. See chapter 8, "Best Practices," for more information on this subject.

3.1.3—Texture Warp Mode
Let's try a few of these Warp Modes in action:

The three sts_dt_synth Clips on the Synth 1 Track sound a bit grainy, and with all the percussion going on in this Track so far, something smoother might sit better in the mix.

11. In the Mixer, click on the Synth 1 Track's Solo button ("S"), which will isolate the sound coming from this Track.

12. Highlight all three Clips at once by selecting the first one and [shift-clicking] on the last one, or by clicking-and-dragging a box around all of them at once.

In the Clip View you will again see a reduced set of adjustable parameters for multiselected Clips, but the Warp Mode controls are still available.

13. Pull down the Warp Mode selector and select Texture, which makes sense, given the tonality of these Clips.

Already the sound is clearer and smoother. When you choose Texture mode, you will see two new parameters become available: Grain Size and Flux. Click-and-drag these variables up and down and listen to the quality of the sound change. You can also double-click on the boxes and type in these values directly. I found a pair of settings that I thought worked well together:

14. Set a Grain Size of 75, and a Flux of 20.
15. Unsolo the Track by clicking on the Track's Solo button again and listen to the adjustments you made to the Clips on Synth 1 in context with the other Clips.

3.1.4—Beats Warp Mode

Next, let's work on the breakdown drums:

16. Select your newest Clip, the Beat_reaktored Clip on the Beats Track. Solo the Track and play the Clip.

The Warp Mode is set to Beats. There are a number of parameters to work with here. First, let's explain the three Transient Loop modes, the box in the lower-left corner where you can choose one of three icons. When Live has to stretch a rhythmic Clip to a length longer than its original length, the Transient Loop modes provide several ways of dealing with the space that gets inserted between the rhythmic sounds:

- Off—The first icon, an arrow pointing to a vertical line, is a mode in which each segment of the sound plays and then silence gets inserted in the gaps.
- Loop Forward—In this mode, each sound segment plays and then Loops forward if more audio is needed to fill in the gap before the next segment.
- Loop Back and Forth—The final mode plays each rhythmic segment and then plays the segment backward to fill in any gaps as needed.
- The Transient Envelope value box to the right of the Transient Loop modes pull-down controls the size of the crossfades used in conjunction with the different Transient Loop modes. This value can tighten or loosen the envelope of your stretched rhythmic audio.

Pic. 3d: The three Transient Loop mode icons.

17. While the Clip plays back, cycle through the Transient Loop modes while adjusting the Transient Envelope value and hear the differences. Also, try some radical adjustments to the Transpose dial while doing this to get some wonderfully strange rhythms!

Next, scroll through the Granulation Resolution pull-down options. These control how note values get preserved when applying these stretching algorithms. The default setting of Transients preserves sudden amplitude changes instead of a fixed grid, and often this setting produces the most transparent, natural stretching results. The other settings can create some wild results, especially in conjunction with the Transpose dial.

18. Try each of the Granulation Resolution settings while varying the other settings, including Transpose. Notice which combinations you like.

19. When you have fully explored all that Beats Warp Mode has to offer, set the Warp Mode to Re-Pitch.

3.1.5—Re-Pitch Warp Mode

Re-Pitch mode is a special case among the Warp Modes, because it is not attempting to preserve the pitch while stretching the length. Instead, as mentioned earlier, in this mode pitch and speed are linked much like a record player: When you slow the audio down, the pitch also comes down, and when you speed the audio up, the length gets shorter and the pitch goes up.

In this case, with your Beat_reaktored Clip, the tempo has been slowed down quite a bit, from 90 to 60 bpm (because you doubled the original Clip tempo). With the rest of the Warp Modes, Live must find ways to insert additional samples into the audio and attempt to still sound natural (or not) while preserving its original pitch. But with Re-Pitch mode, Live just plays the Clip back slower and lets the pitch follow as needed. Because no new samples need to be inserted, often Re-Pitch mode sounds the most natural and least glitchy. As long as you don't mind the pitch changing, that is!

20. You can either leave this Clip in Re-Pitch mode or go back to Beats mode and use settings you liked there.

3.1.6—Tones Warp Mode

Next, let's work with the bass sound a bit:

21. Multiselect all the MT_Bass Clips on the Bass Track.
22. Change all the bass Clips' Warp Modes to Tones.

The Tones mode has an additional parameter known as Grain Size. Tones mode uses small divisions of the sound known as "grains" for stretching, and varying the grain size will produce different results. In this particular Clip, playing with the grain size can diminish the clicky double attack heard on some of the notes.

23. Try varying the Grain Size value. I liked a setting of 42 for the grain size on this Clip. A medium-small grain size seems to match the quick, sharp attack of these Clips.

In my opinion, none of the Clips we've used so far in this piece would benefit from the Complex or Complex Pro Warp Modes, but go ahead and try them on some Clips to hear what they sound like if you want to. Be sure to revert to the original mode when you are done, because the Complex modes eat up your computer's resources, and we have a lot yet to do in this Project before we are done. Conserve where possible!

24. Save your Set by pressing [cmd-s/ctrl-s].

Exercise 3.2—Warp Markers

Clip tempo synchronization and transposition are two very cool uses of Live's Warp engine, but they are not the only uses. The following two exercises will show you two more very powerful and very useful techniques that use the Warp functionality to its full potential.

Every musician misses a beat now and again. Maybe you are playing your instrument and your performance is flawless, save for that one wrong note or instance of bad timing. Or perhaps you are trying to work with two drum Loops that you like, and they almost go together except for that last fill at the end. Well, using this next tool, Warp Markers, you can stretch and shrink digital audio as though it were a piece of chewing gum! You can use it correctively to fix a performance that isn't quite perfect, or creatively to make a piece of audio do something completely unnatural.

Almost all modern DAWs have some type of audio audio-stretching tool at this point, but not only was Ableton Live one of the very first not only to have it, but Live also has the easiest-to-use interface and the highest-quality audio-stretching of any DAW I have tried. Warp Markers represent Ableton Live at its best.

In the next three exercises, we are going to explore three techniques of corrective timing to accomplish the same thing: Warp Markers, Quantization, and Grooves.

3.2.1—Warp Markers Defined

Do It! Time to work with Warp Markers. Here are two ways to get started:

- You can continue from right where you left off at the end of Exercise 3.1 and use Save As... to save the Set as My Exercise 3.2.als, or
- You can open Exercise 3.2.als from the supplied Sets in Book Content > Exercise Sets, and then perform a Save As... and save your Set as My Exercise 3.2.als.

Let's fix that sloppy bass line we've been putting up with for several chapters! It has quite a bit of swing, which is fine, but it doesn't fit perfectly with the timing of the two main drumbeats. Let's improve the timing a bit:

1. Click on the first instance of the MT_Bass Clip in the third Slot on the Bass Track to bring up its Clip View.
2. Now click on the Sample box's Sample Display arrow to ensure that you are in Sample Display mode and not the Envelope Editor.

Look closely at the waveform in the Sample Editor area. At either end of this Audio Clip you will notice a yellow box in the gray bar above the waveform. These are two Warp Markers, and they are added to any Clip that has Warp enabled in the Sample box. In essence, these two Warp Markers delineate the start and end of the Warped Clip, and allow Live to stretch it to fit the Set's global tempo.

Also notice that directly above the start of each note there is a little vertical white line in the gray horizontal bar between the waveform and the Loop Brace. This is known as a "transient," and it indicates a sudden change in amplitude in the waveform. Live designates these as "transients" because transients often present an ideal location to Warp audio from since they typically indicate the start of a new note or drum hit.

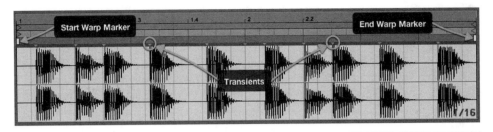

Pic. 3e: Transient indicators and Start/End Warp Markers.

Place your mouse pointer over one of these small white transient marks. A new gray shape appears above the waveform. This is known as a Pseudo Warp Marker, and its purpose is to suggest where you might create an actual Warp Marker. Let's do that.

3. Place your mouse pointer over the transient of the third bass note in this ten-note phrase at 1.2.3. When you see the Pseudo Warp Marker appear, double-click on it. It turns yellow. You have just made your first Warp Marker!

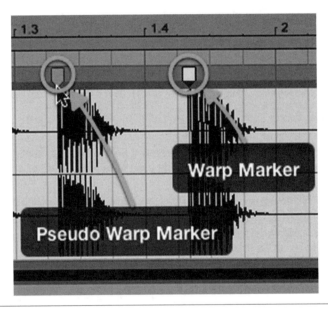

Pic. 3f: A Pseudo Warp Marker and a Warp Marker.

4. Drag this Warp Marker left or right and notice what happens to the audio waveform. Drop the marker somewhere far from where it started, and play back the Clip. You can even move the Warp Marker while the Clip is playing.

More than likely, you have made the timing of the MT_Bass Clip quite a bit more awkward than the way it was to begin with, but you should now have a sense of the power of a Warp Marker. You can pick any point on the waveform and stretch it in either direction, either subtly or to extremes.

Notice that as you move your new Warp Marker, the ends of the Clip do not move because they are anchored to the timeline by their own Warp Markers. Think of the waveform as a rubber band, and each Warp Marker as a pin that you can use to "pin down" the audio, or move to stretch the audio. As you'll see, using multiple Warp Markers together you can correct one section's timing while leaving the rest untouched.

5. Undo your Warp Marker moves by using [cmd-z/ctrl-z] or going Edit > Undo Move Warp Marker(s). Do this as many times as needed until the Warp Marker is back where it started.

3.2.2—Correcting Timing with Warp Markers Snapping to a Grid

This Clip has ten bass notes in it, and the second five are nearly identical to the first five. The first three notes in each bar sound okay, timing wise. It's the fourth and fifth notes that feel a little loose. Before we can move them, however, we need to "pin down" the notes on either side that we don't want to move.

6. We already have a Warp Marker at the third bass note. Double-click on the transient at the beginning of the sixth note as well, so that when we move the fourth and fifth notes that are out of place, the two on either side (whose timing we already like) do not move.

Note your Snap to Grid value in the lower right corner of the Sample Editor. Use [cmd-1/ctrl-1] or [cmd-2/ctrl-2] to increase/decrease the grid value until it reads 1/16, which represents a grid size of 16th notes. Alternately, you can ctrl-click/right-click on the Sample Editor waveform area and set the grid to Fixed Grid: 1/16.

7. Now double-click on the transients above the fourth and fifth notes in the phrase to create Warp Markers for them. Play with the timing of these two notes by moving their Warp Markers left or right. Notice that the Warp Markers snap to the 16th-note grid as you move them.

3.2.3—Correcting Timing with Warp Markers and Snap to Grid Off

While you are moving the fourth and fifth notes, you will still hear the ninth and tenth notes that are out of place. When you find settings that you like for the first half of the Clip, go ahead and correct the second half of the Clip. You could start by double-clicking on the transient above the eighth note to anchor it, the way we did in the first half, but let me show you a great shortcut:

8. Place your mouse pointer above the transient above the ninth note (second from the end). This time, hold down [cmd/ctrl] and double-click.

Live not only creates a new Warp Marker where you clicked, but it also creates one at the transients that are on either side of it. This is a big time-saver when you want to move a single note relative to the notes before and after it. (The end of the Clip at 3.1.1 is already anchored by a Warp Marker, so you do not have to add one after the tenth note.)

9. This time, turn the grid snapping to Off by pressing [cmd-4/ctrl-4] or go Options > Snap to Grid (which will toggle it to Off).

10. Move the ninth and tenth notes to timings that you prefer. As you move the Warp Markers this time, you will notice that they do not snap to the grid, and you can choose any locations for the notes freely. The timings you choose do not have to be the same as the timings in the first half of the Clip unless you want them to be.

These are the timings that I chose:

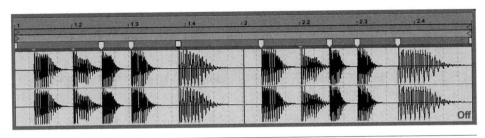

Pic. 3g: MT_Bass note timings cleaned up with Warp Markers.

Now the MT_Bass Clip sits better with MT_Beats and Lighttribal.

11. Save your Set by pressing [cmd-s/ctrl-s].

Exercise 3.3—Quantizing an Audio Clip with Warp Markers

If you have worked with MIDI note data before, you are likely aware of a function called Quantization that moves the recorded notes that you played to the nearest note value of your choosing. But did you know that in Ableton Live you are able to Quantize audio? If your eyes just bulged and your jaw is now hanging open, then you are having the same reaction I did when I saw this next feature in action for the first time.

Quantization is a process of tightening the timings of notes that you played, moving them closer to a predefined grid of your choosing. Originally a function developed for MIDI note data, the geniuses over at Ableton have found a way to apply that same concept to digital audio, greatly streamlining the process of tightening up a loose recording. After the last exercise using Warp Markers, this kind of functionality is the next logical step.

3.3.1—Applying Quantization to an Audio Clip

Get ready to work with Quantization. Here are two ways to get started:

- You can continue from right where you left off at the end of Exercise 3.2 and use Save As... to save the Set as My Exercise 3.3.als, or
- You can open Exercise 3.3.als from the supplied Sets in Book Content > Exercise Sets, and then perform a Save As... and save your Set as My Exercise 3.3.als.

Let's clean up that same MT_Bass Clip, this time using Quantization. First delete your previous Warp Markers:

1. Select the same first MT_Bass Clip on the Bass Track that you just finished working on.
2. In the Sample View, click on one of your Warp Markers to select it.
3. Select all of the Warp Markers by pressing [cmd-a/ctrl-a].
4. Delete them by pressing [delete].
   Great. Back to where we started. Now:
5. To bring up the Quantize Settings, do one of the following:
- Press [cmd-shift-u/ctrl-shift-u].
- Go Edit > Quantize Settings.
- [Ctrl-click/right-click] on the Sample Display waveform area and choose Quantize Settings from the contextual menu.

A small window comes up that asks you which grid value you would like to "Quantize To" and what "Amount" of Quantization you would like to have applied.

6. Set the Quantize To value to 1/16 and the Amount to 100% (if they are not already set at those values).

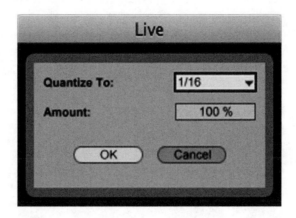

Pic. 3h: The Quantize Settings dialog box.

7. Press OK.

Your MT_Bass Clip now looks something like this:

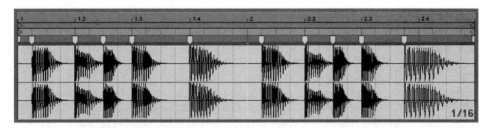

Pic. 3i: The MT_Bass Clip after 16th-note Quantization.

Live has made a new Warp Marker on every transient and then moved each Warp Marker 100 percent of the way to the nearest 16th-note grid divider. Play the Clip. Each bass note falls more rigidly on the beat. However, I'm not sure I like it that "straight."

8. Undo the previous Quantize function by pressing [cmd-z/ctrl-z] or going Edit > Undo Quantize Audio.
9. Hit [cmd-shift-u/ctrl-shift-u] to bring the Quantize Settings dialog box up again. This time leave Quantize To on 1/16, set the Amount to 50%, and hit OK.

Play the Clip. It definitely has more swing than when the Amount was set to 100%. But the syncopation is still a bit awkward. In the Sample Editor, zoom in on any of the notes. Live has moved each of the notes halfway to the nearest 16th-note grid division, which does preserve some of the Clip's swing while still tightening the timing.

10. Undo the last Quantize function by pressing [cmd-z/ctrl-z] or going Edit > Undo Quantize Audio.
11. Hit [cmd-shift-u/ctrl-shift-u] to bring the Quantize Settings dialog box up again. This time set Quantize To at 1/8 and the Amount at 100% and press OK.

Every note has been moved 100 percent to the nearest 8th-note grid division. This sounds pretty stiff on the first three notes of the phrase, but the fourth and fifth notes are now more in time with the rhythm Tracks. Can we have the best of both worlds? Yes! Let's try once more:

12. Undo the previous Quantize function by pressing [cmd-z/ctrl-z] or going Edit > Undo Quantize Audio.
    This time, before you Quantize, select which notes you want to Quantize.
13. Hover your mouse pointer over the top half of the waveform at 1.3 (bar 1, beat 3). (Clicking in the lower half of the waveform will play the Clip, and we don't want to do that.)

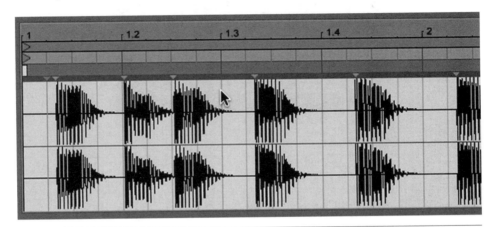

Pic. 3j: The mouse pointer over the top half of the waveform at 1.3.

14. Click here and drag a selection to the right until you get to 2.1.2. You should have just selected the fourth and fifth notes of the Clip. It should now look like this:

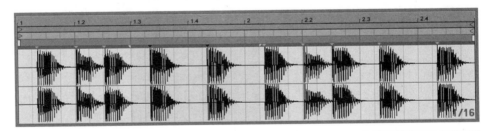

Pic. 3k: 1.3.1 to 2.1.2 selected in the Sample Editor on the MT_Bass Clip.

You could press [cmd-shift-u/ctrl-shift-u] to bring the Quantize Settings up again at this point, but we already know that we want to use 1/8 and 100% as our settings. If you want to reuse the previous Quantize settings, you can do this:

15. To reuse your previous Quantize settings, press [cmd-u/ctrl-u] or go Edit > Quantize.
    Only the fourth and fifth notes are Quantized because of your selection.
16. Repeat the same two steps for the ninth and tenth (last two) notes of the Clip: select the notes and Quantize them with the same settings.

Play the Clip. This sounds pretty good too. The bass still has a little bounce to it, and yet the loosest four notes are now right on the beat divisions. If you wanted to, you could still nudge the notes off the beat slightly to better match the groove of the drums.

Important! Why Undo each previous Quantization before entering new settings? Because Quantization is iterative, meaning that if you Quantize a Clip by 50% and then you Quantize it again with the same settings, you have, in effect, Quantized the Clip by 75% (50%, plus 50% of the remaining 50% equals 75%). Additionally, if you Quantize a Clip to 16th-note divisions at 100%, and then Quantize again to 8th-note divisions at 100%, this will change the note placements twice, since not every 16th note is an 8th note. But if you Quantize to 8th-note divisions first, and then Quantize to 16th-note divisions, the notes will not move the second time, because every 8th-note division is already on a 16th-note division. Keep practicing with this until it becomes clear in your mind.

17. Undo your Quantization once more until you are back to having no Warp Markers.

We are going to use this same Clip for Grooves in the next section, which I think you will find is be the best method so far for what we are trying to accomplish.

18. Save your Set by pressing [cmd-s/ctrl-s].

Exercise 3.4—Grooves and the Groove Pool

Thus far you have seen how to Warp an Audio Clip by adding your own Warp Markers for corrective timing, or using Quantization to automatically move your notes closer to an evenly spaced grid value. But what if we wanted to have the rhythmic timings of one Audio Clip move closer to the timings of another Audio Clip instead of a fixed grid? What if you could take one Clip's rhythmic timings and apply it to several other Clips so that their timings would be more alike and sound better together? This is exactly what Grooves are for. If you understand Warping and Quantization, Grooves are, again, the next logical step.

3.4.1—Extracting a Groove to the Groove Pool

Do It! Are you ready to work with Grooves? I thought so! Here are the usual two ways to get started:

- You can continue from right where you left off at the end of Exercise 3.3 and use Save As... to save the Set as My Exercise 3.4.als, or
- You can open Exercise 3.4.als from the supplied Sets in Book Content > Exercise Sets, and then perform a Save As... and save your Set as My Exercise 3.4.als.

Since you are by now very familiar with your MT_Bass Clips, let's use them once again. Rather than Quantize the bass Clips with a fixed grid, instead apply the Groove of the beats to the MT_Bass Clips. This will ensure that their timings are brought closer together.

To begin, let's make sure that you are starting from a blank canvas:

1. Bring up the Sample Editor for the same first MT_Bass Clip.
2. Ensure that there are no additional Warp Markers besides the first one at 1.1.1. Delete any others that you see by double-clicking on them.
   Now, let's extract the Groove from the MT_Beats Clip.
3. To extract this Groove, do one of the following:
- [Ctrl-click/right-click] on the first MT_Beats Clip and choose Extract Groove(s), or
- Highlight the first MT_Beats Clip by clicking on it and then go Edit > Extract Groove(s).

This will take a moment, which a progress bar conveys. When it is finished, do the following:

4. To apply this Groove to all the MT_Bass Clips simultaneously, first multiselect all the MT_Bass Clips in the Clip Grid one of the following ways:
- Click on the first MT_Bass Clip on the Bass Track and then [shift-click] on the last of the three Clips.
- [Cmd-click/ctrl-click] sequentially on all the Clips until they are all selected.
- Click-and-drag a box around all of these Clips at once (but be sure not to select any neighboring Clips on other Tracks).
   The Multi-Clip View will be displayed in the Detail View at the bottom of your screen.
5. In the Clip panel (all the way to the left), open the Clip Groove selector pull-down menu and select the MT_Beats Groove.

Pic. 3l: The Clip Groove Selector pull-down menu.

Launch Scene 3, called Add Bass. You will notice that many of the MT_Bass notes are more closely aligned to those of the MT_Beats Clip's. It's a subtle difference, but you can toggle the Groove selector back and forth between None and MT_Beats to hear the shift.

You'll continue to refine this in the upcoming Groove Pool section.

3.4.2—Auditioning Grooves from Live's Library with Hot-Swapping

Live also comes with a smattering of Grooves for you to work with that are stored in Live's Library. You could bring the Library's Grooves folder from the Browser fairly easily, but let me show you an even faster way using a button that you will find throughout the program called the Hot-Swap button.

6. Multiselect all three of your Postwarvar Clips on the Synth 1 Track and locate the Clip Groove selector again in Clip View. Instead of selecting a Groove from the pull-down menu, click on the Groove Hot-Swap button (which looks like two arrows chasing each other) just above the pull-down menu.

Pic. 3m: The Groove Hot-Swap button in the Clip box.

Clicking on a Hot-Swap button allows you quickly preview a series of presets from the Library in real time while your music is playing. There are many other areas of the program that use Hot-Swap, including Audio Effects, MIDI Effects, Racks, and Instruments. As long as the Hot-Swap button is lit, you can continue to preview presets as much as you like, and they will be hot-swapped for the one you had previously selected. When you find the one you want, you simply deselect the Hot-Swap button and keep working. You can even modify the preset from there if you wish—a preset is just a starting point for your creativity.

When you select the Groove Hot-Swap button, Live immediately opens the Grooves folder in the Library where you can audition and select one of the preinstalled preset Grooves that ship with the program. They are broken into folders based on where the Groove came from: some are Grooves from other programs and some are sampled from classic hardware Devices such as the MPC and SP1200 folders. Different genres of music and beat-making hardware machines are known for their unique swing, or groove. Ableton has done the homework to bring all of these Grooves to your fingertips. Thanks, Ableton!

7. Open one of the Groove folders and double-click on one of the Grooves to apply it to the three Postwarvar Clips.

   Note that the Hot-Swap button remains lit in the Clip box.

8. Double-click on another Groove file, or use the up/down arrows to select and the [enter] key to apply the Groove to hear its effect on these three Clips.

You can do this while the Clips play to speed up the process. You may want to solo the Synth 1 Track so that you can hear the subtle differences. You may hear no change at all when applying some Grooves, since their timings may be quite similar to the Clip you are working with.

9. After you have tried a few Grooves from a few different folders, look in the Logic folder for a Groove called Logic 16 Sub Up 55 and apply it to your Clips.

This one has a nice pulse to it. You will notice that some Grooves, such as this one, contain Velocity information as well as timing information, and you will hear the volume for the Clips change as well as the swing when it is applied. You will learn more about Velocity when we work with the Groove Pool in a moment.

10. Deselect the Hot-Swap button in the Clip box to keep this Groove.

3.4.3—Groove Pool Parameters

There are several more controls for further tweaking these Grooves in the Groove Pool window.

11. To see the parameters for these new Grooves, open up the Groove Pool by doing one of the following:
- Press [cmd-opt-g/ctrl-alt-g].
- Go View > Browser > Groove Pool.
- In any Clip's Clip Groove pull-down selector, choose the last entry, Open Groove Pool.
- Click on the Groove Pool Show/Hide button at the bottom of the Browser.

Pic. 3n: The Groove Pool Show/Hide button in the Browser and the open Groove Pool.

You may have to stretch your Browser divider out a ways to see all of these available columns of the Groove Pool.

The Groove Pool represents a series of controls that globally modify how each of your Grooves is applied in real time. Changing a Groove's settings will affect the playback of all the Clips in your Set that have this Groove applied to it. Very powerful and very cool.

Let's have a look around:

- Groove Name—The Groove Name lists all of the Set's current Grooves that you have extracted from Clips or imported from the Library. A Groove that is no longer assigned to any Clips is grayed out, but may still be modified or deleted.
- Base—This is the timing resolution that determines which notes of your applied Grooves will be included in the "grooving" process.
- Quantize—This control will apply a grid Quantization to the Grooved Clip before applying the Groove timing adjustments. This value is a percentage amount of Quantization to be applied, exactly like the Quantization Setting's Amount field. The grid value for this Quantization is derived from the Base value mentioned above. By default, 0% Quantization is applied. Sometimes this value can help clean up a very loose performance before the swing of the Groove is applied. If you turn the next field, Timing, down to 0%, no amount of Groove is applied to your Clips, and this field becomes a simple nondestructive grid Quantize amount, which can be quite handy.
- Timing—The Timing value represents how much of the Groove's timing is applied to the Clips that reference it. The default is 100%. If applying a Groove seems to distort or diminish a Clip's impact, try taking this value down until you like the sound again.
- Random—This interesting control introduces an amount of randomness to your new timings after the Quantization and/or Groove timings have been applied. This can add a

bit of "humanness" to your Clips. I like to use this particularly on percussion Clips, such as conga or tabla Loops, so they don't feel so stiff and stagnant.

- Velocity—Here is another intriguing parameter. Keep in mind that a Groove is simply a MIDI Clip with timing and velocity information that has been played in, or extracted from, an audio recording. You can even drag a Groove file onto a MIDI Track and see its timing and velocity values. When a Groove is made from an audio recording, the amplitudes (volumes) of the individual transients that are extracted are translated into MIDI velocity information, so that not only is the amount of swing information preserved, but so are the individual note dynamics. Therefore, the Velocity field in the Groove Pool allows you to impose the velocity information of the Groove onto your Clips. The default is 0%, but when you bring this up to 100%, all of the Groove's velocity information is applied to its associated Clips. Note that this field also goes down into negative values, which imposes inverse velocity information: notes that were loud in the Groove will now be quiet in your Grooved Clips, and quiet notes will be louder. You can achieve a kind of "MIDI sidechain velocity compression" with negative velocity values.
- Amount—This is a global value that affects Timing, Random, and Velocity values for all the Grooves in the Groove Pool. The default of 100% simply passes all of the values as they are currently set. A lower value scales all three of those parameters to smaller values. The Amount value also goes up to 130%, scaling and exaggerating all of the Groove's parameters that much more. Want the Groove of your song to gradually increase or suddenly disappear? Automate this parameter! Or assign it to a knob! Fun!

Play with each of these values and notice the subtle timing shifts that occur to the Clips that these Grooves reference. Here are some values I liked that you might try:

12. Set the following values in the Groove Pool:
- MT_Beats: Base = 1/16, Quantize = 10%, Timing = 100%, Random = 0%, Velocity = 40%
- Logic 16 Sub Up 55: Base = 1/16, Quantize = 0%, Timing = 50%, Random = 10%, Velocity = 40%

3.4.4—Committing Grooves to Clips

Grooves are applied as timing modifications to a Clip on playback, so you will not see the new Groove's timing information displayed in the Sample Editor when you select a Groove in the Clip Groove selector. However, if you want to apply the Groove to your Clip as a series of Warp Markers, click on the Commit button in the Clip box. Live inserts Warp Markers as needed to achieve the new timings much the way the Quantize Audio function did in the previous section, but this time using the selected Groove's timing grid rather than a fixed, evenly spaced grid. Two things to note when using the Commit Groove button:

- When you use the Commit button (described below) to apply the Groove timings permanently to your Clips and you have set your Velocity value to something other than 0% in the Groove Pool, the Groove's velocity information is translated onto your Clip as a Volume Clip Envelope, which you can than further adjust.
- After committing a Groove to a Clip, the Clip's Clip Groove selector is reset to None, so you are not continuing to additionally apply the same Groove on playback as well. You may still select and commit additional Grooves if you so choose.

Pic. 3o: The Commit Groove button in the Clip box.

Do It! Let's try it!

13. Select all of your MT_Bass Clips in the grid.
14. In the Clip box of Clip View, ensure that the current Groove being applied to the Clips is still MT_Beats.
15. Click on the Commit button.

Look in the Sample Editor window: new Warp Markers have been added and the timings of the bass Clips have been adjusted. If you switch back and forth between this Clip's waveform and the waveform of the MT_Beats Clip, you will notice that the Warp Markers you just applied to the bass Clips match the most prominent amplitudes of the MT_Beats Clip's waveform. In essence, you have imposed the MT_Beats Clip's timings onto the rhythm of the MT_Bass Clips, bringing their grooves closer together; this is a subtle, but profound transformation that will go a long way to making your Clips "lock together" and mix more easily.

16. Save your Set!

Summary

- Live's warping engine is what makes Clip tempo synchronization and transposition possible.
- By doubling or halving a Clip's Seg. BPM value, you can instruct Live to play a Clip back at twice or half its original tempo relative to the Set's tempo.
- Live offers a number of different Warp Modes that can either make the Warping of a Clip sound more natural or seriously strange!
- Each Warp Mode has a series of additional controls that can further refine that mode's Warping tonality.
- In addition to a Clip's start and end Warp Markers, which are responsible for making a Warped Clip play back at the Set's current global tempo, you can add your own Warp Markers to further modify a Clip's internal timing in the Clip's Sample Editor.
- Live notates a Clip's transients (sudden changes in amplitude) as small, white marks above the Clip's waveform in the Sample Editor. These transient marks are Live's suggestions for logical places to add additional Warp Markers.
- When you mouse over a transient, a gray "ghost" of a Warp Marker appears, which is known as a Pseudo Warp Marker. Pseudo Warp Markers can easily be turned into Warp Markers by double-clicking on them or simply by clicking on them and moving them.

- Warp Markers will snap to the current grid value if Snap to Grid is on, or move about freely if Snap to Grid is off.
- Audio Clips in Live can be Quantized to a fixed grid value. Quantizing audio will insert a series of Warp Markers on the Clip's transients to facilitate this.
- An Amount value in the Quantize Settings dialog box allows you move a percentage of the total distance to the nearest grid division.
- A portion of an Audio Clip can be selected and then Quantized, which will then affect the timings within only the given selection.
- A Groove is a MIDI Clip that contains timing and velocity information. These Clips can be created by hand in a MIDI editor, played in via a MIDI controller, extracted from the timing and amplitude of an audio recording, or selected from Live's Library of Grooves. This timing and velocity information can then be applied to another Audio (or MIDI) Clip, thereby imposing the timing of one Clip on one or more other Clips.
- Once a Groove has been applied to a Clip, it appears in Live's Groove Pool where various Groove-specific and global parameters can be modified.
- Grooves extracted from other Audio and MIDI Clips also appear in Live's Groove Pool. These can be saved to Live's Library for future use.
- Grooves affect the timing of a Clip's notes on playback and are nondestructive until they are Committed by pressing the Clip's Commit button in the Clip View. Committing a Groove to a Clip will create one or more Warp Markers in that Clip to impose the Groove's timing on the Clip.

Chapter 4

ARRANGEMENT VIEW

Congratulations on making it through Session View and Clip View! You may be feeling overwhelmed with information at this point, but your perseverance is about to pay off as you move into Arrangement View.

Session View is what fundamentally sets Live apart from other DAWs, and if you can get comfortable working with it, you will be capable of improvising arrangements, soundscapes, and even entire DJ sets without a lot of effort. Its power lies in having all those Clip variations right there at your fingertips, ready to be triggered in any order you like with the click of a button.

And yet, there are times when you need to commit to a linear arrangement and sculpt one of those infinite possibilities into a finished product. Maybe that means verses, choruses, and a bridge. Perhaps you need to make a score for a video. Or you could be recording your DJ set to make a promotional demo. When you need to commit to a linear timeline, that is when it is time for Arrangement View. Arrangement View functions just the way the traditional horizontal timeline that most DAWs offer does, plus it has a few unique tricks, as you are about to see!

Understanding Arrangement View and how the two Views work together will be the focus of this chapter.

Exercise 4.1—Making an Arrangement with Session View Clips

This next feature—recording your Session View Clips into an Arrangement—is the feature that made me quit my previous DAWs for good. Prepare for a jaw-dropper!

4.1.1—Preparing to Make an Arrangement

Do It! Here are two ways to get started:

- You can continue from right where we left off at the end of Exercise 3.4 and use Save As... to save the Set as My Exercise 4.1.als, or
- You can open Exercise 4.1.als from the supplied Sets in Book Content > Exercise Sets, and then perform a Save As... and save your Set as My Exercise 4.1.als.

When you open Exercise 4.1, you are looking at the (by now extremely familiar) Session View layout of Audio Clips and Tracks, plus a few more that I have added at the bottom. I have been laying these Clips out in this intentional way so that stepping through the Scenes in a top-to-bottom fashion would suggest a rough song structure. However, keep in mind that you can still trigger any Clip you like at any time. Take some time and play through the Clips and Scenes until you are familiar with what they sound like and how they work together.

Do It! When you feel as though you know your way around the Session grid reasonably well, do the following:

1. Click on the Stop All Clips button to make sure that all of your Clips are stopped.
2. Also, double-click on the Stop button in the Control Bar at the top of the screen. You will notice that the Bars, Beats, and Sixteenths numbers to the left of the Control Bar now read 1.1.1. These numbers are called the Arrangement Position, and we will delve deeper into what they mean later in this chapter.
3. Now, do one of the following to enable the Global Record button:
- Click on the Global Record button in the Control Bar.
- Press F9 (In some cases your operating system may have these function keys mapped to other non-Live system tasks. If this is the case, you can unprogram them in your System Preferences so you can use them with Live instead if you wish.)

Although you have just enabled a button called the Global Record button, you are not actually going to record any audio; you are going to record an Arrangement. So don't worry about attaching a microphone just yet.

4. Launch the Intro Scene by clicking on its Launch button on the Master Track. You are now recording.
5. Click through the Scenes, or use your [up/down arrows] and the [enter] key, in a way that feels right to you. Feel free to additionally click on individual Clips on the Session View Clip grid as you see fit.

Note the 1 Bar Global Quantize value: New Clips and Scenes will begin at the next bar after you click on them.

6. When you have stepped through all the Set's Scenes, stop recording—and playback—by doing one of the following:
- Press the [spacebar].
- Click on the Stop button in the Control Bar.

You might be thinking "I'm confused: I don't see anything new. What did I record just now?" Fear not:

7. Press the [tab] key to switch to Arrangement View, or click on the Arrangement View Selector in the upper right of the interface.

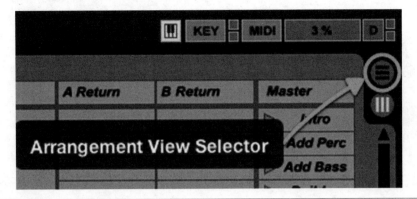

Pic. 4a: The Arrangement View Selector.

Behold your new Arrangement!

Although you enabled a button called the Global Record button, you did not record any new audio. Instead, Live "recorded" all your Session View gestures into a layout here in Arrangement View!

8. Double-click on the Stop button to return to the beginning of the timeline of the Arrangement.
9. In the Control Bar, press the red Back to Arrangement button to disable it.

This will stop all playing Clips in the Session View Clip grid so that only the Clips in the Arrangement are playing. We will discuss the purpose of this button later in the chapter.

10. Press [spacebar] or click on the Play button in the Control Bar to begin playback.

You are now listening to the arrangement you "recorded" from Session View the way you performed it a minute ago. You can still make changes to what you just did, perfecting it, or adding to what is already there. Amazing!

Although we just used this feature to "record" an arrangement of this basic song, you can use this same feature to record an entire Session View performance for as long as you like. Want to capture an hour-long DJ set? No problem: hit Global Record and go! When you finally stop recording, everything you just did will be notated perfectly in Arrangement View down to the subtlest gesture. Did you make a mistake while performing? Of course not, you are a superstar! But if you had made a mistake, you could find it in Arrangement View and correct it. Amazingly powerful.

Let's take a look at a few of Arrangement View's unique features:

The Arrangement View Interface

A vast majority of the layout and controls of Arrangement View are replicas of everything you are already familiar with in Session View, but with a slightly different look. Let's get oriented. To have your screen look like the screenshot below, make sure that all of your interface sections are being shown in the View menu. Below is a diagram and list of the areas that are changed from Session View:

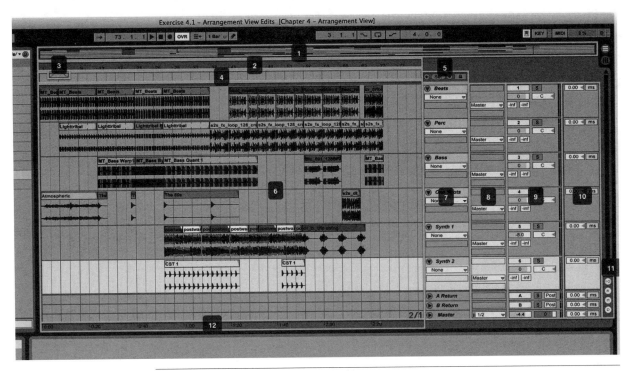

Pic. 4b: Arrangement View with all Show/Hide buttons enabled.

- 1. The Overview
- 2. The Beat ruler
- 3. The Arrangement Loop controls
- 4. The Scrub area
- 5. The Marker Creation/Navigation area
- 6. The Arrangement area
- 7. The Track Name area
- 8. The In/Out section
- 9. The Mixer section
- 10. The Track Delay section
- 11. The Show/Hide buttons
- 12. The Time ruler

Notable Arrangement View differences from Session View include the following:

- The first thing you may have noticed about Arrangement View is that the orientation of your Tracks and controls has rotated 90 degrees counterclockwise. The Track controls are now on the right instead of at the bottom, and instead of a vertical Track full of Clips, Tracks now flow from left to right and Clips now have durations on the timeline.
- Each Track has a small, triangular Fold/Unfold button in the Track Name box used to quickly minimize or unminimize any Track. Tracks may also be manually resized by clicking-and-dragging on the horizontal gray line between Tracks in any of the visible right-hand columns such as the Track Name, In/Out, or Mixer sections.
- The Track Name column has two new pull-down selectors on it. These are used for Automation selection and editing. The follow-up book to this book, Sound Design, Mixing and Mastering in Ableton Live, has a detailed chapter on mix automation.
- The Mixer controls, such as Track Volume, Track Pan, and Track Sends are minimized to numerical values to save space. Note that the Sends are now merged with the Mixer

controls in Arrangement View, and cannot be hidden unless you minimize the entire Track.

- Although the Sends Show/Hide button is no longer present in Arrangement View, you still have Return Tracks that can be shown or hidden, and these Tracks function exactly the same as in Session View. You'll learn more about Sends and Return Tracks in chapter 5, "Using Audio Effects."
- The Master Track has the same controls, although the Master Pan and Preview/Cue dials have been reduced to numerical values to save space.
- The Detail View area at the bottom of the screen functions exactly the way it did in Session View, and you can still view and change Clip View properties of any Clips on the timeline. Note, however, that once a Clip exists in both Views, they are two separate Clips: adjusting the properties of a Clip in Arrangement View will not affect the same Clip in Session View, and vice versa.

Additionally, there are a few new controls in Arrangement View to be aware of:

- Notice that there is now a Beat ruler and Scrub area at the top of the Arrangement area that functions exactly like the one in the Sample Editor for zooming and scrolling the entire arrangement. As well, there is a Time ruler at the bottom of the Arrangement area, and you can scroll with it, but not zoom.
- Although you have not needed or used it yet, it is useful to now notice the Overview area above the ruler (double-check that the Overview is visible by going to the View menu and making sure that Overview is checked). Available in both Views, this miniature representation of your entire Arrangement allows you to both navigate your whole song and see at a glance which part of your Arrangement you are currently viewing in the Arrangement window via the Zooming Hot Spot black box. The Arrangement Overview functions exactly like the Clip Overview (discussed previously in chapter 2, "Audio Clips and Session View"). Try it!
- The Loop/Punch In/Out Brace works similarly to the Clip Loop Brace, and its controls are found at the top of your Live interface to the right of the Draw Mode switch. In addition to allowing you to Loop a portion of your arrangement on the fly, it has the added functionality of being a punch-in/punch-out range selector for recording to a specific spot or length on the timeline.
- Although there are currently no Locators in this Arrangement yet, they appear in the Scrub area, and the controls for making and navigating them are above the name of the first Track. We'll work with Locators briefly in this chapter.
- Similarly, although you do not have any Time Signature Change markers yet, they can be inserted into the Arrangement View Scrub area to automate time signature changes.

4.1.2—Using Session View and Arrangement View Together

The Arrangement View is a highly intuitive interface, especially if you have ever worked with another linear timeline DAW application before. You will pick it up in no time. But one of the more challenging concepts to grasp is how the two Views work together. Just because we have recorded our Session View performance into an arrangement in Arrangement View does not mean that we are done with Session View! It is still a creatively fertile environment for exploring new Clips and Scenes. And when you come up with something new in Session View, you can still translate those new ideas into Arrangement View.

Important! Fully understanding this next exercise is central to mastering Ableton Live. So take it slow and easy. Don't worry about making a mess of your Set in the following steps—I'm going to have you open an arrangement I've prepared for you in the next exercise anyway. The important thing is that when you are done you understand the relationship between Session View and Arrangement View.

By now your Set should contain a nice assortment of Audio Clips on the Clip grid in Session View and a rough arrangement made from the same Clips in Arrangement View. Let's get reacquainted:

11. Enable the Overview for both Session View and Arrangement View (if it is not already) by pressing [cmd-opt-o/ctrl-alt-o] or going View > Overview in both Views. Note that while the Overview functions the same way in both Views, you have the option of independently hiding or showing it in each View.

12. In the Arrangement View, disable the following sections to reclaim some screen real estate: Track Delay, In/Out, and Returns.

13. Double-click on the Zooming Hot Spot box on the Overview to zoom all the way out so you can see your entire arrangement. You could also use the minus key [-]or the magnifier on the timeline to achieve the same thing.

14. Double-click on the Stop button to return the Arrangement Position (in the Control Bar) back to 1.1.1. This assures that you will begin playback from the first bar of your timeline.

15. Press the [spacebar] to begin playback.

In Arrangement View the playback indicator moves along the timeline showing you where you are in the arrangement. Similarly, the Overview presents a miniature version of the same thing.

16. With Live sill playing, press [tab] to switch to Session View.

In Session View, the Overview shows you a similar story, but besides that, nothing much is going on: none of your Clips on the Clip grid are playing.

Important! While both Views currently share the same Audio Clips, only the ones in Arrangement View are currently playing. Clips played back in Arrangement View will not launch their respective Clips in Session View.

17. Press the [spacebar] to halt playback.

18. In the Browser, navigate into Book Content > Sounds to Sample > Drum Loops and find the audio file dr_drLoop_chukfunk_130. Drag this file onto one of the open Clip Slots on the Beats Track, preferably below all your other Audio Clips on the Track. Rename this Clip as Chunkfunk.

19. Press the [spacebar] to start playback again. Notice that playback starts at 1.1.1 again from the top of your arrangement.

20. Now, with the arrangement still playing, launch the Chunkfunk Clip on the Beats Track in Session View.

When Chunkfunk launches, you will now hear the Chunkfunk Clip instead of whatever was previously playing on the Beats Track. While still playing back, press [tab] to switch back to Arrangement View and notice that the Beats Track is grayed out. The MT_Beats and Beat_reaktored Clips are still there on the timeline, but the Chunkfunk Clip you launched in Session View supersedes the playback of these Clips in the Arrangement.

Important! Clips launched in Session View during playback will supersede any Clips already playing on the same Track in the Arrangement View.

21. While still in Arrangement View, press [spacebar] to halt playback.

Note that the Beats Track is no longer grayed out.

22. Press [spacebar] again to restart playback.

Note that the Track grays out again, and you are still hearing Chunkfunk instead of MT_Beats.

23. With playback still rolling, hit [tab] to switch back to Session View.
    Notice that Chunkfunk is still playing.
24. Click on any open Clip Slot's Stop Clip button on the Beats Track to stop the Chunkfunk Clip's playback.

Now Chunkfunk is no longer playing, but MT_Beats in the Arrangement does not resume playing. Nothing is playing on the Beats Track!

25. [Tab] back to Arrangement View. The Beats Track is still grayed out, even though nothing else is playing in Session View.

Did you notice that the button in the Control Bar that you clicked on earlier has turned red again? That is the Back to Arrangement button.

26. To reenable the Arrangement View Clips on the Beats Track, disable the Back to Arrangement button in the Control Bar.

Pic. 4c: The Back to Arrangement button in the Control Bar.

Important! Launching Clips (or triggering Clip Stop buttons) on a Track in Session View will suspend that Track's playback in Arrangement View and light the Back to Arrangement button. Arrangement View Clips on this Track will not play again until the Back to Arrangement button is disabled. Disabling this button tells Live to resume playing the arrangement Clips as they are currently laid out on the Arrangement View timeline, and stop any Clips playing in Session View.

The takeaway here is that you can still launch Clips in Session View to try them out with your present arrangement, and they will take the place of whatever was previously happening on that Track. When you are through trying them out, you can resume your previous arrangement with the Back to Arrangement button. Make sense?

4.1.3—Overdubbing from Session View to Arrangement View

Let's say that after auditioning Chunkfunk in the previous exercise, you decided that you liked the new Clip enough to want it in your arrangement. Now let's do the same thing, but this time actually overwrite our Session View gestures onto the arrangement in Arrangement View:

27. In Session View, click on Stop All Clips.
28. Double-click on the Stop button to return the Arrangement Position to 1.1.1.
29. Click on the Global Record button or press [f9].
30. Click on the Play button or press [spacebar].
31. At some point in the arrangement, when you are ready to hear the new beat, launch the Chunkfunk Clip.
32. [Tab] over to Arrangement View and see your new Clip overwriting on the Beats Track.
33. When you would like to stop adding the Chunkfunk Clip and return to the previous arrangement's Clips on the Beats Track, do one of the following:
- Click on the Back to Arrangement button to resume the previous arrangement.
- Click on the Global Record button again (or hit [f9] again) to suspend recording.
- Click on Stop or press [spacebar] to stop recording. You will still need to disable Back to Arrangement to hear the Beats Track.

You now have Chunkfunk on the Arrangement View timeline. Because you hit "record" before starting playback, Live "overdubbed" your Session View gestures onto the Arrangement.

Let's do this one more time but on a grander scale!

34. Enable the Global Record button with [f9].
35. Start playback.
36. Launch any Clips from any Track on the Clip grid whenever you want to modify the arrangement you are listening to.

Any Track that you launch a Clip on will now be overdubbing over the current arrangement.

37. Stop Global Record using any of the previous three methods.
38. Switch over to Arrangement View and check out the results.

Everything you just did was recorded into the Arrangement. Click somewhere in the Scrub area to play back what you just recorded.

Are we having fun yet, or what?

39. Save your Set by pressing [cmd-s/ctrl-s].

Exercise 4.2—Editing in Arrangement View

Arrangement View is where you will sculpt the broad overview and subtle nuances of your song. The tools for doing so are easy to learn and work with, so let's jump in.

4.2.1—Adding Locators to the Arrangement

Do It! For this next exercise, I have made an arrangement that I would like you to use (if you want to come back to your current Set for use with later exercises, that is fine):

- Open the Set Exercise 4.2.als from the supplied Sets in Book Content > Exercise Sets, and then perform a Save As... and save your Set as My Exercise 4.2.als.

Arrangements will get increasingly complex as they build in length and number of Tracks. The first thing to do is familiarize yourself with this new arrangement I've prepared and put up some "signposts"—known as Locators—to remind you where you are in the song.

1. Play through the entire arrangement and listen for the major musical shifts.
2. When you are done, double-click on the Stop button to return to the beginning of the timeline, 1.1.1.
3. Go Create > Add Locator. A triangle with the number 1 appears in the Scrub area.
4. To rename the Locator as Intro, do one of the following:
- Click once on the Locator's triangle and then press [cmd-r/ctrl-r], as you would to rename any object in Live.
- Right-click on the Locator's triangle and choose Rename from the contextual menu.

Pic. 4d: A new locator at 1.1.1.

You can double-click on a Locator to start playback from that point. For now, you are simply using Locators as an arrangement divider to remind you where you are in the arrangement.

5. [Ctrl-click/right-click] in the Scrub area at bar 5. From the contextual menu, choose Add Locator.

This is another way to add a Locator. Notice that when you do it this way, Live prompts you to rename the Locator right away.

6. Name this Locator as Add Perc.
7. Repeat this process to add a locator called Add Bass at bar 13.
8. Add more Locators at bars 21, 29, 39, 49, and 73.
9. Rename the Locator at bar 21 as Buildup, but instead of pressing [return], press [tab] instead: Live jumps you to the next Locator for renaming.
10. Rename the Locator at bar 29 as Main Groove1 and press [tab].
11. Rename the Locator at bar 39 as Breakdown1 and press [tab].
12. Rename the Locator at bar 49 as Breakdown2 and press [tab].
13. Rename the Locator at bar 73 as Main Groove2.

You now have Locators defining the major changes in your arrangement.

4.2.2—Working with Clips in Arrangement View

Working with Clips in Arrangement View is almost exactly the same as working with Clips in Session View. Double-click on any Clip on the Arrangement View timeline and Live will present you with the same Clip View properties that you are used to working with from Session View. Let's explore a pair of brief examples to demonstrate these similarities and slight differences.

14. Click on the Lighttribal Clip that starts at bar 5 on the Perc Track. This brings up the Clip View properties in the Detail View.
15. In the Sample box for this Clip, raise the Clip Gain slider to –3 dB. (You will have to double-click on the gain value and type it in to get it exactly to –3 dB.)

You have raised the gain of this Clip, and this Clip only! All the other Clips on the Track—including the one directly after it that is otherwise exactly the same—remain unaffected. This simply reiterates the idea that Clip View properties affect only the selected Clip.

16. Click on the Clip s2s_dt_synth_mornvar1_A#m, which currently begins at bar 57 on the Synth1 Track. Now hold down [shift] and click once on the Clip dr_fx_trip string directly below it on the Synth2 Track to multiselect them both.
17. In the Clip View properties, you now see the message "2 Audio Clips With Different Lengths Are Selected in 2 Tracks" letting you know that you have multiple Clips selected. Lower the Clip Gain slider to –3 dB. (Again, you will have to type it in to get it exactly to –3 dB.) Both of the Clip's Gain values have been reduced to –3 dB at the same time.

This is simply to show that you can still adjust properties of multiple Clips at the same time in Arrangement View.

Let's try changing two other Clip View properties that work in a logical yet interesting way.

18. Click on the dr_fx_trip string to bring up its properties.
19. Make sure that you are in Sample Display mode (not Envelope Editor mode) by clicking on the Sample box's title bar.
20. Do one of the following to lengthen this Clip's Clip and Loop Length to four bars:
- In the Sample Editor, click-and-drag the Loop Brace's Loop End to 5.1.1.
- In the Sample box, set the Loop Length to 4.0.0 and the Clip End to 5.1.1 by typing in these values in their respective boxes.

As you do this last step, notice what happens to the waveform of the Clip on the Arrangement timeline: the regularity of how often this Clip plays is halved, and it now repeats every four bars instead of every two.

21. Do one of the following to change the Clip's Start point:
- In the Sample Editor, click-and-drag the Clip Start triangle to the right two beats to 1.3.1.
- In the Sample box, set the Clip's Start point to 1.3.1 by typing in this value in the Start boxes.

Notice what this does to the Clip's Waveform in the Arrangement timeline as you move the Clip Start value: the waveform slides backward on the timeline, but the Clip's beginning and ending boundaries remain in place. You are not changing the start time of the Clip on the timeline—rather you are changing the start point of the Clip's playback within the already defined Loop. Cool!

4.2.3—Making Edits in Arrangement View

When a sculptor starts a new sculpture, he or she first selects the stone that they want to work with, and then remove the largest chunks before with a large chisel before zeroing in on the finer details. I like to think of the previous exercises in a similar fashion: select the Clips that you want to work with in Session View, lay them out in Scenes, and then record a rough arrangement onto the Arrangement View timeline. This exercise will deal with how to take your rough arrangement and slowly remove and refine what is there, creating new, detailed nuances for your song in progress.

Let's start with learning about a few new intuitive functions that quickly and easily modify your arrangement and how to use the Arrangement Loop settings.

Toward the end of the timeline, the arrangement shifts back into the original motif, but only very briefly. Let's preview this, and then extend it in case we decide to build upon it later:

22. At bar 73, click on the dr_drLoop_chukfunk_130 Clip on the Beats Track to select it.
23. Do one of the following to Loop the selection:
- Press [cmd-l/ctrl-l].
- Go Edit > Loop Selection.

The Arrangement View Loop Brace moves to surround the selected bars, and the Loop Switch lights at the top of the screen to indicate that Arrangement Looping is now on. Press the Play button to hear these two bars Loop repeatedly. Despite the fact that you selected only one Clip region, Looping on the Arrangement View timeline Loops all the Tracks on this segment of the timeline.

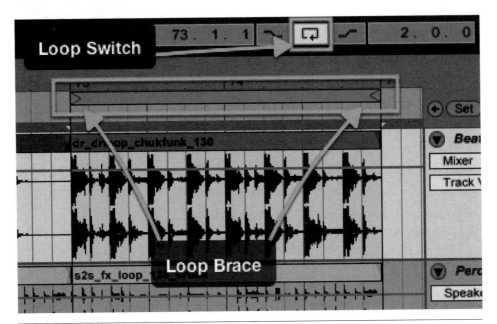

Pic. 4e: The enabled Loop switch in the Arrangement Loop controls and the Loop Brace.

The Arrangement Loop is separate and different from individual Clip Loop settings. The Arrangement Loop is for Looping a section of the timeline. There are many reasons you might want to do this: to focus playback on a section of the song you are working on, or perhaps to replay a section of a song while you are playing it live. Since you'll be using the Arrangement Loop repeatedly throughout this section, let's take a moment to understand its controls.

Notice the numbers to the left of the Loop switch that read 73.1.1. These numbers indicate the start time of the Looping region in the Loop Brace—in this case, bar 73, beat 1, sixteenth 1.

The numbers to the right of the Loop switch represent the current length of the Loop Brace, in this case 2.0.0 or exactly two bars.

These three Clips sound pretty good together. We should have them play longer than just two bars in our arrangement. Here are two easy ways to lengthen a series of Clips:

24. Place your mouse over the right-hand edge of the colored title bar of the dr_drlopp_ chunkfunk_130 Clip. You will see your cursor turn into the square Resize bracket, like this:].

25. When you see the bracket, click-and-drag the right-most edge of the Clip to the right to bar 81.

26. Click on the Loop switch to disable the Arrangement Loop and play the whole 16 bars you have just created.

You have just resized the length of the Clip on the timeline. Since the Clip has Loop enabled in the Clip View properties, you can extend the length of this Clip indefinitely and it will simply repeat. Note the small, vertical line in the colored Clip name recurring every two bars that indicates where the Loop restarts.

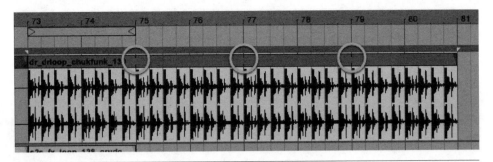

Pic. 4f: The Loop Start indicator in a Clip on the Arrangement View timeline.

Important! Notice that any selection you make or Clip boundary you modify snaps to the current grid value. The controls used for modifying the grid in Sample Edit View work in exactly the same way here:

- Pressing [cmd-1/ctrl-1] narrows the grid, as does choosing Options > Narrow Grid.
- Pressing [cmd-2/ctrl-2] widens the grid, as does choosing Options > Widen Grid.
- Pressing [cmd-3/ctrl-3] toggles triplets on and off, as does choosing Options > Triplet Grid.
- Pressing [cmd-4/ctrl-4] toggles the grid on and off, as does choosing Options > Snap to Grid.
- Pressing [cmd-5/ctrl-5] fixes the grid size, regardless of zoom level, as does choosing Options > Fixed Grid.

Note that the current Arrangement grid size is displayed in the lower right corner of the Arrangement window on the Master Track.

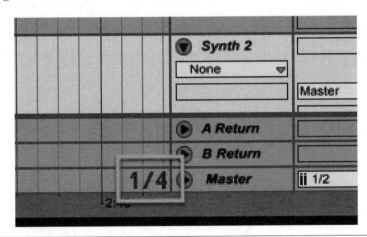

Pic. 4g: The current Arrangement Snap to Grid value.

You can do this kind of resizing to multiple Clips at the same time to save time:

27. Click on the s2s_fx_Loop_128_crude Clip on the Perc Track so that it is selected. Now press [shift-click] on the Clip below it, MT_Bass Quant 1, to multiselect them.
28. Place your cursor over the right-hand edge of the Clip name of either of these two selected Clips as you did before. You will see the Resize bracket, which looks like this:].

29. When you see the Resize bracket, click-and-drag the edges out to bar 81 to match the previous Clip on the Beats Track.

Here's another way to extend a Clip, or in this case, a series of Clips:

30. Click once on the dr_drlopp_chunkfunk_130 Clip at the top to select it.

Notice that when you click on this Clip the whole eight bars of it is selected, since it is one contiguous, Looping Clip.

31. Do one of the following to duplicate the Clip:
- Press [cmd-d/ctrl-d].
- Go Edit > Duplicate.

Live duplicates the Clip, creating a copy to the right of it, further down the timeline. Note that it is a discrete, separate Clip rather than an extension of the length of the Clip. Extending a Clip or duplicating it sounds exactly the same when played back. The only real difference is that with duplicated Clips, you can change the Clip View properties of one of the duplicated Clips to differentiate them.

Let's do this to your two other Clips, but in a slightly different way.

If you click-and-drag within a Clip, you can make a selection within the Clip instead of selecting the whole thing. You can then perform operations on just that portion of the Clip.

32. Click-and-drag downward in the Beat Time ruler at the top to zoom the timeline view until you can see the numerical divider for bar 80.

33. Put your cursor on the waveform of the s2s_fx_Loop_128_crude Clip exactly at bar 80.

34. Click-and-drag right and down until you have selected the first half of bar 80 on this Track and the MT_Bass Quant 1 Clip on the Track below. It should look like this:

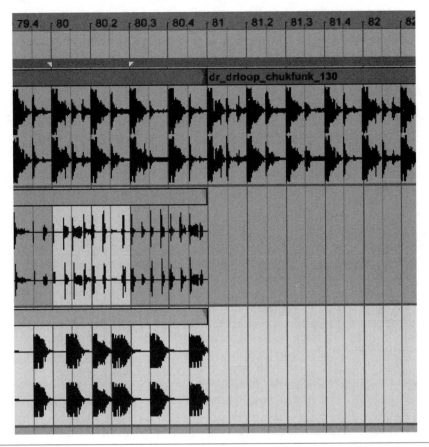

Pic. 4h: The first two beats of two adjacent Clips selected.

35. Without changing your selection, execute the Duplicate command nine times (see how much easier the keyboard shortcut is?). It now looks like this:

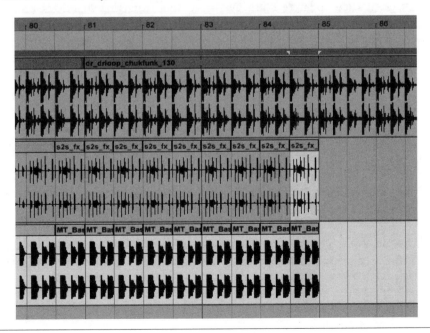

Pic. 4i: Nine duplicates of two beats of two Clips.

36. Now go through and delete alternating Clips of each to make a checkerboard like this:

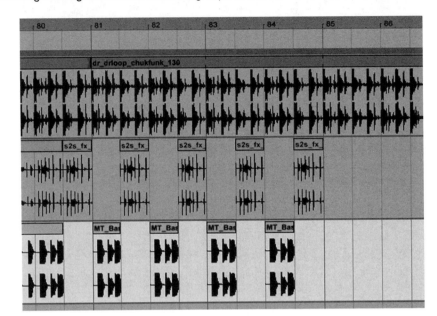

Pic. 4j: Checkerboarded Clips.

As you can see, the Duplicate function works on a selection of Clips, or a selection within Clips. It's a quick way to repeat a phrase. Sometimes extending a Clip is the way to go, sometimes duplicating is more useful if you need individual Clip chunks. You will discover for yourself what works best for what you are trying to do.

4.2.4—Global Timeline Edits

Now let's try our hand at functions that operate on a whole section of the timeline globally. Here's a common situation: Perhaps when recording your Clips from Session to Arrangement View you were a little overhasty when triggering your Scenes, and so a section such as the Main Groove did not get the chance to establish itself fully before you moved on to the Breakdown1. This is easily remedied with Duplicate Time.

For the Duplicate Time and Delete Time functions, all you need to do is establish a selection of time that you wish to duplicate or delete, and thankfully you only need make this selection on a single Track rather than a gigantic multiselection across potentially dozens of Tracks, which can be cumbersome. Here are two easy ways to accomplish the same thing:

The simplest way is to find a Clip that spans exactly the region you wish to duplicate or delete and click on it to quickly select that time range for your operation:

37. Click on the MT_Beats Clip starting at 29.1.1 and ending at 39.1.1 on the Beats Track to select it.

This Track conveniently spans one full cycle of the 10-bar Postwarvar synth figure that is Looping on the Synth1 Track at this point. Repeating this entire section would make a lot of sense.

38. To Duplicate Time across all Tracks, do one of the following:
- Press [cmd-shift-d/ctrl-shift-d].
- Go Edit > Duplicate Time.

When you Duplicate Time, Live duplicates the bars on all Tracks in the range selected (regardless of whether they are all selected or not) and creates enough time to insert the duplicated bars.

Now we have two identical repetitions of the Main Groove section. I like this better.

Sometimes, however, you do not have a Clip that is exactly the length and placement needed to make such a convenient one-click selection of what you need to duplicate or delete. In these instances, you must make your own selection.

For example, take the Buildup1 section: the bass bends upward in pitch for just under six bars. Yet the Buildup1 section is currently eight bars long, so the bass builds to a crescendo and then just levels off for at least two extra bars, which lessens the excitement that the buildup is trying to create. Let's remove those two extra bars:

39. On any Track—even an empty one—click-and-drag a selection from 27.1.1 to 29.1.1. You may have to zoom in a bit to see exactly where 27.1.1 is.
40. To Delete Time and remove these bars across all Tracks, do one of the following:
- Press [cmd-shift-delete/ctrl-shift-delete].
- Go Edit > Delete Time.

Delete Time removes the selected bars across all Tracks (regardless of whether they were selected) and moves all the later Clips in your Arrangement to the left to fill in the gap.

By comparison, let's make a few standard (nonglobal) deletions:

41. Click on The 80s cymbal crash on the One Shot Track at 37.1.1 to select it.
42. To delete it, do one of the following:
- Press the [delete] key.
- Go Edit > Delete.
- [Ctrl-click/right-click] on the Clip and choose Delete from the contextual menu.

The Clip is deleted, and no other Clips are moved as a result. This is the delete function you will likely use most often.

Sometimes it is useful to combine several Clips into one for easier arrangement use. Try this:

43. On the Synth1 Track, click-and-drag from bar 27 to 37 to select one repetition of the Postwarvar Clips. To Consolidate these Clips into one big Clip, do one of the following:
- Press [cmd-j/ctrl-j].
- Go Edit > Consolidate.
- Press [ctrl-click/right-click] on the selected Clips and choose Consolidate from the contextual menu.

The three Postwarvar Clips combine into one new Clip.

44. With the new consolidated Clip still selected, duplicate it twice.

Then again, at other times, it is necessary to have a Clip, or a part of a Clip, separated from the rest for processing. This is easily done:

45. On the Beats Track, select 55.4.1 to 57.1.1 of the Beat_reaktored Clip. Do one of the following to Split this range of the Clip into a new Clip:
- Press [cmd-e/ctrl-e].
- Go Edit > Split.
- Press [ctrl-click/right-click] and select Split from the contextual menu.

This region of the Beat_reaktored Clip is now its own Clip and has its own Clip View properties. Let's apply a new setting, Reverse, that you have not used until now:

46. Double-click on the new Clip from 55.4.1 to 57.1.1 on the Beats Track to open its Clip View properties. In the Sample box, click on the Rev. button, which will reverse playback of the Clip.

Pic. 4k: The Reverse button in the Sample box of Clip View.

Moving right along! Now we will use a combination of the above methods to make several more modifications:

47. Using the Clip Resize bracket at the edge of the Clip, click-and-drag the beginning of the Beat_reaktored Clip from 49.1.1 to 57.1.1.
48. Click-and-drag a selection on the Beats Track from 81.1.1 to 83.1.1 (across the end of the Beat_reaktored Clip) and delete this range.
49. Zoom in on the end of the same Beat_reaktored Clip. Click-and-drag a selection from 79.4.1 to 80.1.1 and duplicate this selection (not Duplicate Time!) four times.
50. In the same Beat_reaktored Clip, select the snare from 79.3.1 to 79.4.1. Copy it using [cmd-c/ctrl-c]. On the same Track, click on the grid marker at 82.4.1 to locate your insert point there, and press [cmd-v/ctrl-v] to paste the snare there.
51. On the Bass Track, select bar 66 of the Clip Blu_001_128BPM_Abm and delete it. Delete bar 70 and bar 74 as well.
52. On the Perc Track delete bars 79 through 81 from the s2s_fx_Loop_128_crude Clip.
53. On the Beats Track delete bar 26, the last bar of the Buildup section.
54. On the One Shots Track, copy the cymbal hit at bar 13. Paste it starting at bar 26. Double-click on this new copy at bar 26 to open its Clip View properties. In the Sample box, click on the Rev. button, which will reverse playback of the Clip.

Now it's taking shape! Let's insert a little space at the end of the Breakdown1 to ease the transition back to the Main Groove2:

55. Click on any Track at bar 83 to set your insert point there. (Using a Track with no Clips at that point in the song, such as the One Shots Track, might be easiest.) To Insert Time, do one of the following:
• Press [cmd-i/ctrl-i].
• Go Create > Insert Time.
   A small dialog box comes up asking you how many bars you'd like to insert.

56. Type a "2" into the second box (or press the [up arrow] once) so it reads "0.2.0." Hit OK. Live inserts two beats of silence across all Tracks at the insert point.

4.2.5—Automating the Time Signature

Rather than have the Main Groove2 section start in the middle of a bar at 81.3.1, let's change the time signature of bar 81 so that the two new beats you just inserted are their own measure of 2/4.

57. Here are two ways to make a time signature change:
- [Ctrl-click/right-click] on the grid divider at bar 81 in the Scrub area just below the Beat Time ruler and choose Insert Time Signature Change from the contextual menu.
- Click on the grid divider where you want the time signature change to occur on any Track in the Arrangement View to locate your insert point, and go Create > Insert Time Signature Change.

When you have done either of these, a new time signature change marker appears in the Scrub area, and a small rename box awaits your new time signature value. Type 2/4 into the box and press [enter].

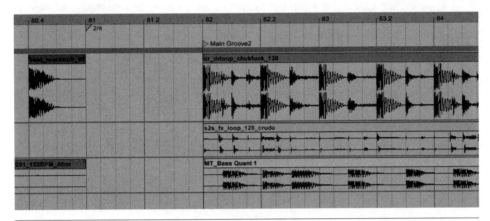

Pic. 4l: A Time Signature Change marker.

All the bars after the new Time Signature marker will now be counted in 2/4, and that is not really what we want: we want just one bar of 2/4. Repeat the above process at bar 82 to insert a new marker to change the time signature back to 4/4 at that point.

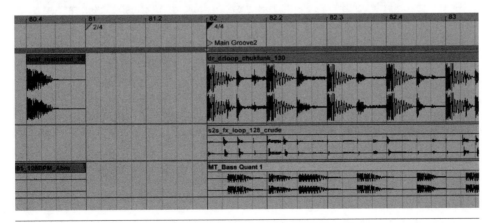

Pic. 4m: Two Time Signature Change markers.

Let's fill in the measure of 2/4 to bring these two parts together:

58. Move the snare on the Beats Track from 80.4 to 81.2. (You will have to zoom in to see this level of detail. Adjust your grid to quarter notes if that helps.)
59. Extend the s2s_fx_Loop_128_crude Clip that starts at 82.1.1 back to start at 81.1.1.
60. Extend the dr_fx_trip string on Synth2 that currently ends at 81.1.1 so that it ends instead at 83.1.1.

4.2.6—Automating the Tempo

Virtually every parameter in Live can be automated in Arrangement View. This is done with a simple Breakpoint Envelope editing technique just like Clip Envelopes. We're going to do it to the Tempo parameter right now, but this technique will work on almost any parameter! For more information on mix automation, see the companion book, Sound Design Mixing and Mastering in Live.

Do It! Perhaps the breakdown section could use a slight drop in tempo to make it stand out even more:

61. To bring up the global tempo breakpoint envelope, press [ctrl-click/right-click] on the Global Tempo box and choose Show Automation from the contextual menu.

A red horizontal line appears on the Master Track, and some new controls show up under the Track name:

Pic. 4n: The Master Track Tempo automation controls.

The red line is a graphical representation of the timeline's tempo, with higher tempos at the top of the Track and lower tempos toward the bottom. Because the tempo currently does not vary (staying at 120 bpm for the entire song), the line is flat and has no variations.

The two new value boxes on Master Track are the Tempo Range Minimum and Maximum fields. These values determine the "bookends" of the range of tempos displayed on the Master Track. It is not necessary for you to change these values, but using them to narrow the range of possible tempos can make detailed tempo automation edits a lot easier.

62. Set the Tempo Range Minimum to 115 and the Tempo Range Maximum to 120 to "zoom" the tempo editing range.
63. On the Master Track, drag a selection from bar 57 to 81.
64. Anywhere within the selection, click-and-drag the red tempo breakpoint envelope downward to the bottom of the Track but no further, and release it.

Live creates four new breakpoints on the tempo automation envelope.

65. Drag the upper left breakpoint at bar 57 back to bar 55, keeping the breakpoint at the top of the visible Track range, which is 120 bpm.

This creates a gradual slowdown in tempo from bars 55 to 57 from 120 bpm to 115 bpm. At bar 81, the tempo instantaneously reverts to 120 bpm.

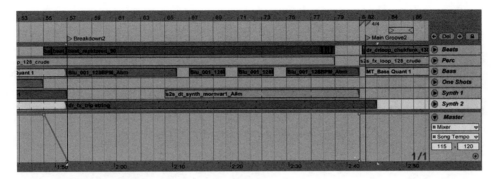

Pic. 4o: The final tempo automation breakpoint envelope.

You can use any combination of breakpoints to automate the tempo (or any parameter you like) in this way. Double-clicking on the line will create a new breakpoint, and double-clicking on a breakpoint will delete it.

Play through the entire arrangement. You've come a long way! Don't forget:

66. Save your Set!

Summary

- Arrangement View is a horizontal, timeline-centric view, as opposed to Session View's nonlinear approach.
- You can record a performance from Session View into an arrangement in Arrangement View simply by enabling Global Record and then performing your arrangement with your Clips in Session View. Launched Clips and Scenes will take effect on the next Global Quantize value.
- Arrangement View's mixer has all the same controls in a slightly different configuration.
- Clips on the timeline in Arrangement View have Clip View properties just like the ones in Session View.
- The Arrangement Loop Brace functions in a similar fashion as the Sample Editor's Clip Loop Brace, except that its function is to Loop a range of time in your Arrangement.
- If you launch Session View Clips while playing back an arrangement in Arrangement View, the newly launched Session View Clips will supersede anything already playing on the same Track(s) from Arrangement View. To return to the arrangement as it is laid out in Arrangement View, click on the Back to Arrangement button in the Control Bar.
- Locators may be added to the timeline and renamed. This can be helpful for identifying sections of a song.
- Clip View properties of Arrangement View Clips may be changed on one or more Clips at a time, much like in Session View.
- Arrangement View Clips may be modified in numerous ways such as Duplicate, Delete, Copy, Cut, Paste, Split, or Consolidate. They can also be resized with the Resize bracket.
- The entire arrangement can be modified globally with functions such as Duplicate Time, Delete Time, Insert Time, Cut Time, and Paste Time.

- The grid in Arrangement View functions very similarly to the grid in the Sample Editor. It can be narrowed, widened, shifted to triplets, turned on or off, and be fixed to a single value if desired.
- A Clip's playback can be reversed by pressing the Reverse button in the Clip View Sample box.
- Tempo and Time Signature (and most other parameters) can be automated to change over time.

Chapter 5

USING AUDIO EFFECTS

Ableton Live offers a fantastic spread of great sounding audio plug-in effects. Don't let the simple interfaces fool you! These plug-ins can rival many third-party effects. As well, these effects were designed to be used in a live-performance setting and are surprisingly light on your computer's resources, so you can use a lot of them. Now that you have the basics of Live's mechanics under your belt, enjoy diving into these effects. The sound-shaping possibilities here are endless!

Types of Audio Effects

There are many ways to categorize types of effects. I like to divide them in the following way:

- Frequency-based effects: equalizers, tone shapers, filters, frequency shifters, resonators, vocoders, and so on.
- Dynamic-range effects: compressors, limiters, gates, expanders, and so on.
- Temporal/spatial effects: reverbs, delays, choruses, flangers, auto panners, and so on.
- Distortion effects: amp/speaker simulators, tube saturators, overdrives, bit/ sample-rate reductions, and so on.
- Diagnostic tools: These are not effects so much as tools to visualize and measure audio, but they can show up in your DAW as audio plug-ins, and so people sometimes lump them in with effects. They include level meters, spectrum (frequency) analyzers, correlation/phase scopes, tone/noise generators, and so on.

Two Ways to Use Audio Effects

There are traditionally two ways to use an Audio Effect, and this is not just true of Live. These two techniques evolved from years of analog audio engineering throughout the past century of recording, and you will find this methodology replicated in every studio on the planet or DAW on the market.

- You can use effects in series as an insert effect.
- You can use effects in parallel as a send effect.

Insert Effects

When you drop Audio Effects on an Audio Track, they are connected in series. This means that the Audio Clip's signal flows into the first effect on the Track, then the affected audio continues into the second effect, and so on down the line. With an insert effect, only the audio playing on the Track with the effect gets affected. A good analogy for this would be a guitar player using effects pedals: the guitar outputs the clean sound of the guitar, which then goes through a series of effects that change its sound, and arrives finally at the amp where it gets amplified and sent to the speaker. Each of the effects can be bypassed or their order rearranged to modify the quality of the sound you are seeking. After audio passes out of the last effect on the Track, the audio from that Track is mixed together with the audio from the other Tracks at the Master Track, where the audio is output to your sound card and ultimately to your speakers.

Serial Processing with Insert Effects

Pic. 5a: Effects on a Track in series using Track insert effects.

A typical use for an insert effect would be dropping an EQ or a compressor on a Track where it is desirable to color the tone or constrain the dynamics of the entire Track's output.

Send Effects

The second method, known as a send effect, sends a copy of any Track's signal to what is known as a Return Track. You may then insert effects on these Return Tracks in the same way you would an Audio Track. But the result is different from an insert in series on an Audio Track in several ways:

- You can send a variable amount of signal from any number of Tracks to these Return Tracks using a Track's Send dial. For example, put a reverb on one of the Return Tracks, and all your Tracks can share this reverb in differing amounts at the same time.
- In addition to the amount of signal sent over the Track's Send, audio also flows through the Track in the usual way, including any effects that may be there. That is why this is known as processing a Track "in parallel": two versions of the Track are being affected in two different ways at the same time.

The original Track and the Return Track's audio are eventually mixed together at the Master Track, where they are then output to your sound card and speakers.

Parallel Processing with Send Effects

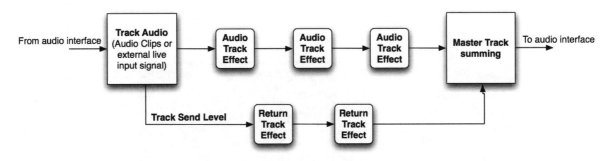

Pic. 5b: Effects in parallel using a Track's send and a Return Track.

A typical use for a send effect would be placing a reverb or delay on a Return Track so that you could apply as much or as little of these effects to any Track you choose using each Track's Send dial.

Master Track Effects

Master Track effects are technically just another use of insert effects, but because they are used on the Master Track, they affect the entire mix. Every sound played through the Master Track will be affected by an effect you put there. It is not uncommon to put an EQ or a compressor on your Master Track to control the overall sound of your entire mix.

I will show you how to apply insert and send effects as you get familiar with a few individual specific Audio Effect Devices.

Exercise 5.1—Applying Audio Effects as Inserts on Audio Tracks

Using Audio Effects is like using spices while cooking: Both are used to enhance flavor, add dimension, and create unique appeal. And just like the use of spices in cooking, there are conventional, traditional ways to use Audio Effects (compressing drums, de-essing a vocal, and so on), and then there are an infinite number of unconventional ways to use (and abuse) them in search of never-before-heard sounds. Both are equally valid approaches, but I believe that knowing some of the rules is helpful when you decide to break them. So we will begin by talking about a few of the more traditional uses of these effects.

In my years of experience as an audio engineer, I have come to the opinion that EQ and dynamic compression are the two most important—and difficult to master—tools in your tool bag. I call them "the salt and pepper of Audio Effects." They are the two tools that you will return to every day for the rest of your audio-engineering career, so get to know them well. EQ and dynamic compression are deceptively simple: one adjusts tone, and the other, volume. Yet the more time I spend with EQ and compression, the more secrets they reveal.

Equalization (EQ)

Equalizers, or EQ for short, are tone-shaping tools. They boost or cut the gain of a particular range of frequencies. They can be as simple as the bass and treble controls on a car stereo or sophisticated algorithms for doing sonic surgery. Returning to the cooking analogy, equalization is the salt of the effects world, insofar as almost any sound could benefit from some of it, yet when overused, it can be harsh and hard to swallow. How much is enough? Like salt, that is a matter of personal taste. But like a great chef, a great mix engineer knows how much is just right.

Live comes with two dedicated EQs: the EQ Three and the EQ Eight. The numbers three and eight refer to the number of frequency bands you can adjust. Let's have a look at both of them.

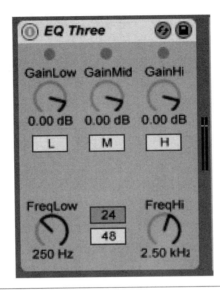

Pic. 5c: The EQ Three.

Important! Note the Device Activator that is present in every Live Device. Think of it the way you would the foot-activated bypass switch on any guitar pedal: disabling it bypasses the effect and sends the unaffected audio through with no change to the next effect in the chain. These switches can be automated in Arrangement View or with a Clip Envelope.

The EQ Three is modeled after the EQ on a DJ mixer, and as such works well as a quick and easy tone shaper for DJ-type applications. The three Gain dials adjust the relative amount of lows (bass), mids (mid-range), and highs (treble) in the affected signal. In keeping with the DJ theme, note the three "kill" switches (labeled L, M, and H) that completely filter out (turn off) the lows, mids, or highs, respectively. These are great for making sudden shifts in tone or isolating a particular instrument you want to feature. Want to hear the hi-hat from this beat with the kick drum from that beat? No problem: drop an EQ Three on both Tracks, and disable the lows and mids on the first Track and the mids and highs on the second Track. Easy.

The bonus feature on the EQ Three is something that I have always wished DJ mixers had: two sweepable crossover points. These are adjusted with the two dials at the bottom, FreqLo and FreqHi. These values define the boundaries between low, mid and high, so you can really tune in the instrument you are after. The 24 and 48 buttons define the slope of the crossover filters. On the 24 setting, the filter slopes downward at a rate of 24 decibels per octave. So if your FreqLo crossover point is 250 Hz (the default) and your mid and high bands are toggled off, the signal's 500 Hz content (one octave above the 250 Hz crossover point) would be turned down by 24 dB, and the 1,000 Hz content (two octaves above the 250 Hz crossover point) would be an additional 24 dB down, or 48 dB lower than normal. At the 48 setting, the filter would slope downward twice as steeply as the 24 dB/octave filter. The slope of the crossover filters will change the sound of the transitions between the bands.

Like all effects, the best way to learn about them is to try them.

5.1.1—Applying an EQ Three Audio Effect to the Beats Track

Do It! Let's get ready to try out some Audio Effects:

- You can continue from right where you left off at the end of Exercise 4.2 and use Save As... to save the Set as My Exercise 5.1.als, or
- You can open Exercise 5.1.als from the supplied Sets in Book Content > Exercise Sets, and then perform a Save As... and save your Set as My Exercise 5.1.als.

Let's apply an EQ Three as an insert effect to the Beats Track and shape the tone of all the Clips that play on this Track. You can do this from Session View or Arrangement View, but since you already have an arrangement made, let's work in Arrangement View for now.

1. Use [tab] to make sure you are looking at Arrangement View.
2. In the Browser click on the first button below the Browser Show/Hide triangle, which is the Live Device Browser.

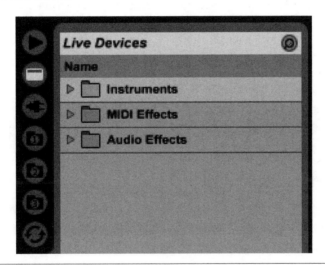

Pic. 5d: The Live Device Browser button and the contents of the Live Device Browser window.

3. The Live Device Browser window contains three folders: Instruments, MIDI Effects, and Audio Effects. If it is not already open, click on the triangle to the left of the Audio Effects folder to show its contents.
4. Scroll down until you see EQ Three in the list of Audio Effects.

There are three ways to add an Audio Effect to a Track. We will try each of them in turn. Here is the first one:

5. Click-and-drag the EQ Three effect from the Browser onto the Beats Track. You may drop it anywhere on the Beats Track that you like: on the Track's name, on a Scene Slot in Session View or on the Beats Track's timeline in Arrangement View. When you let go of the effect, you will see it appear in the Detail View at the bottom of Live's interface.

Important! Up until now we have only used the Detail View area to display Clip View properties. Its other use is to show the Track View, which is where you will work with Instruments, MIDI Effects, and Audio Effects as we are doing presently. You can switch between these two Detail Views by pressing [shift-tab] or by clicking on either the Clip Overview or the Track Detail tabs below and to the right of the Detail View area. Notice that the Track Detail tab shows the Track name (Beats) and a miniature picture of any effects on the Track, in this case, the EQ Three you just added.

Pic. 5e, The Clip Overview and Track Detail tabs.

Okay! We now have an EQ Three on the Beats Track. Let's try working with it.

6. Solo the Beats Track by clicking on its Solo button in the Mixer section.
7. Click on the first MT_Beats Clip on the Beats Track timeline to select it. Press [cmd-l/ctrl-l] to Loop this section of the arrangement.
8. Press [spacebar] to begin playback.
9. Adjust the three Gain dials and hear their effect on the sound of the beat.
10. Toggle the three band switches off and on again to hear their effect on the beat.
11. Leave the L button on and turn M and H off. Adjust the FreqLo dial to change the crossover frequency between the lows and mids.
12. Turn the H button on and turn the L and M buttons off. Adjust the FreqHi dial to change the crossover point between the mids and highs.
13. Turn the L and H buttons off and the M button on. Adjust both the FreqLo and the FreqHi dials to hear the range of frequencies in the mids change. Toggle the filter switch from 24 to 48 dB/octave to hear the steeper filter slope.
14. When you are done experimenting, turn all three L, M and H switches on and set the three Gain dials the way you like them.

Cool! Would you like to return a dial to its default value? Click on it once to select it (you will see four black brackets at the corners of the control, or a black box around the value box), and then press the [delete] key. This works on every dial, slider, and value box in Live.

Important! Note that adjusting the EQ's Gain dials will definitely affect the Track's output gain. Although we think of EQs as "tone adjusters," they definitely affect amplitude (aka gain, or volume) of a Track as well. If you turn the Gain dials up, you can easily send the Track or Master gain into the red, which means that it is clipping and distorting. Keep an eye on your signal levels as you use any Audio Effect.

5.1.2—Applying an EQ Eight Audio Effect to the Perc Track

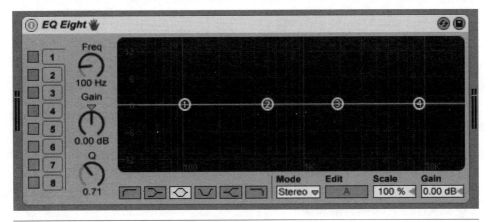

Pic. 5f: The EQ Eight.

The EQ Three paints with a pretty wide sonic brush, which is fine for broad, DJ-type tonal adjustments across a wide frequency spectrum. When a more precise tonal adjustment is needed, it's time for the EQ Eight.

The EQ Eight is a wonderful sound-sculpting tool, offering up to eight adjustable EQ points, each of which can select between six available EQ shapes. By combining multiple EQ points and shapes, you can drastically (or subtly) alter a Track's sonic characteristics.

Do It! To begin with, let's add an EQ Eight as an insert on the Perc Track. Here is the second way to add an Audio Effect to a Track:

15. Click on the Track name that you want to add an effect to, in this case the Perc Track, and then double-click on the effect you wish to add, in this case the EQ Eight.

An EQ Eight is added to the Perc Track, which switches to Track View in the Detail View area and displays the EQ Eight interface.

To begin with, notice the graph across the majority of the EQ Eight. This is a graph depicting frequency from left to right (30 Hz to 22 kHz) and gain from top to bottom (+15 dB to –15 dB). The four numbered circles on the orange line are the first four of eight adjustable EQ nodes. The fifth through eighth nodes start in the Off state by default.

16. In Arrangement View, click on the first Lighttribal Clip on the timeline of the Perc Track. Press [cmd-l/ctrl-l] to Loop this segment.
17. Unsolo the Beats Track and solo the Perc Track.
18. Engage playback.
19. In the EQ Eight, click-and-drag the yellow circle node 1 on the EQ graph. Move it up, down, left, and right. Notice its effect on the sound, and notice the two dials on the left that change as you drag: Freq (frequency) and Gain.
20. With the first node significantly above or below the line, [option-click/alt-click] on it and drag upward and downward. The node stays in place, but the width of the curve widens and narrows. Notice how the dial on the left, called Q, changes with it.

Each of the eight EQ nodes has these same three controls. If you are familiar with EQs, this interface will be immediately accessible to you. If not, you will quickly discern the following:

- The left side is low Freq (bass), and the right side is high Freq (treble).
- Above the line adds Gain, and below the line cuts Gain.
- Q controls the width of the notch.
- You can move the EQ points on the graph, or turn the dials to achieve the same results.
- You can switch between EQ nodes by clicking on their number in the graph or on their Filter Selector in the sidebar by the three dials.
- You can turn a particular node on or off in the sidebar using the orange Filter Activator squares. Use these to disable nodes, or activate nodes 5 through 8 as needed.

EQ Eight Filter Modes

All eight EQ nodes can select between six different filter-shape modes. From left to right, they are as follows:

Pic. 5g: The EQ Eight's Filter mode selectors.

- Low Cut—Also known as a "highpass filter," the low-cut mode is a filter that cuts frequencies below the selected frequency at a slope controlled by the Q dial. Note that moving the node up or down controls Q instead of Gain in this setting.
- Low Shelf—The low shelf is similar to the bass dial on a home or car stereo: the shelf boosts or cuts frequencies below the node. However, unlike the home-stereo bass knob, this shelf has an adjustable frequency dial. You home or car stereo's shelf is fixed. The slope up or down to the shelf is controlled with the Q dial.
- Bell—This filter-shape is the default setting, and allows you to boost or cut a given frequency and neighboring frequencies on either side. Width is set with the Q control.
- Notch—A notch is like a bell filter, but with an infinite negative gain: it strips out the chosen frequency, and the width of neighboring frequencies is set with the Q control. Note that moving the node up and down controls Q instead of Gain in this setting.
- High Shelf—A high shelf is the opposite of a low shelf: it boosts or cuts every frequency above the chosen frequency.
- High Cut—A high-cut filter, also known as a "lowpass filter," is the opposite of a low-cut: it removes all frequencies above the selected frequency at a slope controlled by the Q dial. Note that moving the node up and down controls Q instead of Gain in this setting, just like with the Low Cut filter shape.

You can mix and match as many of each filter mode shapes as you like using different EQ nodes. The effects of two overlapping EQ shapes are cumulative, meaning you can, for example, boost with a shelf while simultaneously cutting a portion of the shelf with a bell.

Do It! Here are some settings that I liked for the EQ Eight on the Perc Track:

21. Set node 1 to a low-cut filter, with a frequency of 202 and a Q of 0.68. This strips out some muddiness in the low end that was clashing with the bass and primary drum Loops.
22. Node 2 is a bell shape. Set it with a frequency of 725, a gain of 8.11, and a Q of 1.45. This brings out the warmth of the congas and helps it to punch through the drum Loops.
23. Set node 3 to a bell (which it started at), with a frequency of 1.58 kHz, a gain of –3.69, and a Q of 1.65. This removes some "honk" in the mids that was annoying and makes room for other sounds in the mix that sound better in this frequency range.
24. Set node 4 to a high shelf, with a frequency of 3.33 kHz, a gain of 8.36, and a Q of 5.92. A little bit of brightness or "air" in the high end gives it some crispness and adds energy to the performance. Although other instruments will also use this range, the congas have short, staccato hits and are panned quite wide, so they don't interfere with anything all that much.

As you can see, equalizing is a process of removing and bringing out certain aspects of a sound to make it sound better and play well with the other sounds. In general, aim to make sounds more interesting, and keep different instruments from clashing or stacking up poorly in a particular frequency range. This is not something you will master overnight. It will take years of practice. Get started!

Dynamic Compression

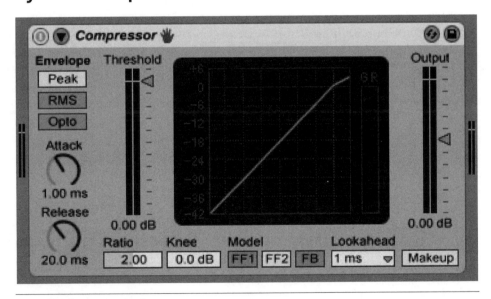

Pic. 5h: The Compressor plug-in.

Dynamic range is the difference between the loudest sound and the quietest sound in a recording. Dynamic compression reduces the dynamic range of a piece of audio, often so that you can turn its overall volume up without it going into clipping. Like using ground pepper, compression can add punch and impact to your Tracks if used correctly. But also like pepper, used incorrectly, it can make a Track overwhelming or leave it lifeless. For most people, using dynamic compression is more challenging than using an EQ.

Imagine listening to a recording of a person who is using a microphone as he gives a lecture. The speaker's volume and distance from the microphone are generally consistent, except in a few places where the speaker coughs. You would like to turn the gain of this recording up, but if you do, the coughing moments will definitely go over into clipping. If you could turn all the loudest parts down—in this case the coughing—you could turn the overall volume up, right? This is exactly what a dynamic compressor does. It reduces dynamic range so you can turn the overall volume up.

Important! You will notice that I tend to refer to this type of gain-reduction effect as "dynamic compression." I do this not only because that is what it truly is, but also to differentiate it from "data compression," such as making an MP3 or using Zip. People often confuse these two types of compression, and they have nothing to do with each other. The first reduces an audio's dynamic range, while the second makes file data smaller.

Live has several dynamics processors, including the Limiter, Gate, and Multiband Dynamics, and even Saturator, Overdrive, and Dynamic Tube do some significant dynamics manipulation. But the one that you will likely use most is the Compressor.

5.1.3—Applying a Compressor Audio Effect to the Bass Track to Add Thickness

Do It! To begin, let's add a Compressor Audio Effect to the Bass Track. Here's a third way to get an Audio Effect on an Audio Track:

25. Double-click on the Track name you wish to add an effect to, in this case, Bass. This will display the Track's Track View in the Detail View area at the bottom of the Live Interface. Having no effects yet, this area is empty except for a message that says "Drag Audio Effects here." Who are we to say no? Drag-and-drop a Compressor from the Live Device Browser onto this area.

26. Click on the first MT_Bass Clip in the timeline on the Bass Track in Arrangement View to select it. Then press [cmd-l/ctrl-l] to Loop this selection.

27. Solo the Bass Track (and unsolo any other Tracks).

28. Play the Looped range.

29. If the Compressor is not showing in Detail View, double-click on the Bass Track name to show its Track View.

Like the EQ Eight, the Compressor has a number of dials and a graphic representation of the values of some of those dials.

30. To begin, click on the Threshold triangle and drag it down until the value underneath the slider reads −17.5 dB.

Several things just happened here, and the net result was that the bass got a lot louder. A dynamic compressor works like this:

- You begin by setting an amplitude (volume) threshold. Any signal that passes above this threshold will be turned down, thus reducing the signal's dynamic range.

- Any signal that goes over the threshold will be turned down at a rate expressed as a ratio of "some number to 1." For example, a ratio of 3:1 means that "for every 3 dB the input signal goes over the threshold, the compressor will output 1 dB." This means that if the threshold were −17.5, like the settings above, and an incoming signal were

−11.5 (6 dB over the threshold), the compressor would output the signal at −15.5 dB (2 dB over the threshold, or three times less). This is what the graph in the center of the Compressor Device depicts. The net result is a gain reduction of 4 dB, which is what the G.R. (gain reduction) meter imparts. The larger the ratio setting, the greater the gain reduction for signals over the threshold.

- Since the signal was reduced by 4 dB at the loudest point, you could then safely turn this entire Track up by 4 dB without the risk of clipping. The loudest parts got quieter, and the quietest parts got louder—this is dynamic range reduction.

31. Adjust the threshold and ratio values and note the sound of varying amounts of gain reduction. Notice how less gain reduction sounds quieter but more punchy and dynamic. Notice how more gain reduction sounds consistently louder yet flatter.

Threshold and Ratio are the two most important controls on a compressor, but there are several more controls that also contribute to the overall sound:

- The Attack dial specifies how long it takes for the gain reduction to be applied after a signal has crossed up over the given threshold. Higher settings can let a little of the signal pass through before it gets compressed, which preserves a punchy attack transient.
- The Release dial specifies how long the Compressor will keep the gain reduction applied after the signal has dropped back below the threshold. Lower settings allow the Compressor to recover gain reduction more quickly, while higher settings will keep the signal's output gain more consistent.
- A higher Knee value will round out the threshold, causing a more gradual onset of gain reduction as a signal's gain approaches and crosses the threshold. As the Knee setting rises, gain reduction will gradually start to occur further and further below the given Threshold. This can make the gain reduction sound more natural and less aggressive.
- The Output Gain slider allows you to turn the entire output signal up after the gain reduction has been applied to the loudest parts. The Makeup button, which is engaged by default, does this gain makeup for you automatically. If the loudest signal's gain is reduced by 4 dB, Makeup will add 4 dB automatically. Alternately, you can use the Output Gain slider to set any output value you like.
- The three Envelope Follower mode settings modify how the Compressor measures input gain, thereby emulating the way that various hardware compressors behave. In Peak mode, the threshold responds well to short, sharp transients. RMS stands for "root-mean-square," and in this setting, the threshold responds to a signal's averaged loudness over time, rather than to transients, which is closer to the way our ears work. The Opto (short for "optical") setting is a type of hardware compressor that has a curved release stage, which can often sound more musical on signals benefiting from longer release times (vocals, for example).
- The three Model Types emulate three different compressor types. Generally I like FF2 model for signals with significant bass content and shorter release times. Opposing that, I like the FB model for softer, more legato content or signals requiring a longer release time. The FF1 mode seems to sit somewhere between the other two.
- Finally, the Lookahead value allows the Compressor to analyze the signal at 0, 1, or 10 milliseconds ahead of what you are hearing. Increasing this value will often increase the gain reduction as transients over the threshold are detected earlier.

Adjust any and all of these values, and notice what settings make the bass sound more interesting to you. Take as long as you like. If it isn't entirely clear to you what a setting is doing to the sound, don't worry about it. Compression is a complex task, and you will get better with practice.

Here are some settings I like:

- Threshold: −17.5 dB
- Ratio: 2.67
- Knee: 0.2
- Attack: 16.4 ms
- Release: 6.14 ms
- Envelope: RMS
- Model: FF2
- Lookahead: 0
- Output: −5.61
- Makeup: On

5.1.4—Using a Compressor to Smooth Dynamic Range on the Perc Track

In the previous exercise, we used dynamic compression to fatten a sound that was already fairly consistent in volume: all of the notes of the bass line were being compressed by approximately the same amount. We did this to fatten the impact of the instrument.

Another use for a compressor is to smooth out dynamic range to bring up the quieter details of a sound. If you can turn down the loudest transients in a phrase, you can turn the overall volume up, which brings out the quieter parts you might not have heard before. Let's try this on the Perc Track since the Lighttribal and s2s_fx_Loop_128_crude Clips are quite dynamic presently:

32. Solo the Perc Track.
33. Loop the first of the Lighttribal Clips: click on the Clip from bars 5 to 13, and then press [cmd-l/ctrl-l] to Loop that section.
34. Add a Compressor to the Perc Track using any of the three methods above. Place it after the EQ Eight that is already there.

Important! You can easily switch the order of effects on a Track by simply clicking-and-dragging them by their title bar to where you want them and letting go. You can also choose where in the signal Chain you want to place a new effect by dropping it where you want it when you first add it to the Track. In either case, you will see a vertical yellow bar appear that shows you where the effect will be placed if you let go if it. Try reordering the EQ and Compressor on the Perc Track a few times to get comfortable with this technique. Obviously, the order in which the effects appear on a Track makes a difference as to how the result will sound. For now, place the Compressor after the EQ Eight.

35. Press play. Apply the following settings while the Loop is playing:
- Envelope: Peak
- Attack: 1 ms
- Release: 32.9 ms
- Threshold: −24.1 dB
- Ratio: 3.00

- Knee: 10
- Model: FB
- Output: 2 dB
- Makeup: Off

With these settings, the loudest peaks are turned down significantly (note the orange G.R. meter showing gain reduction), but the quietest parts are unaffected. The result is a less dynamic Track that is more consistent in volume, which allows us to hear more of the quieter parts without the loud parts overpowering.

Important! You will note that the Compressor registers more gain reduction in the first Lighttribal Clip than in the ones that follow. That is because the first Lighttribal's Clip Gain is –3 dB and the others are –8 dB. The important thing to understand here is that the Clip Gain adjustment occurs before a Track's effects chain, so any adjustment of the Clip Gain slider will affect the amount of gain going into all the effects on that Track. This is especially important with the use of compressors, as their threshold setting is relative to the incoming gain of that Track's Clips. If you change a Clip's gain setting, you will also be affecting how much compression is taking place in your Compressor.

Let's see this in action:

36. Engage playback while still Looping bars 5 to 13 and soloing the Perc Track.
37. Double-click on the first Lighttribal Clip that is inside the Looping region to bring up its Clip View properties.
38. Reduce the Clip Gain value to –20 dB. The waveform in the Sample editor diminishes to show the reduction in gain.
39. Now press [shift-tab] (this is a very useful keyboard shortcut) or click on the Track View tab in the lower right corner with the miniature EQ Eight and Compressor on it to switch from Clip View to Track View. You will notice that the Compressor is barely registering any gain reduction.
40. [Shift-tab] back to Clip View. Raise the Clip Gain back to –3 dB. [Shift-tab] back to Track View. The Compressor is working quite a bit harder now.

With the Compressor Threshold remaining constant, you are varying the incoming gain to the plug-in chain, which affects the amount of gain that exceeds the threshold, and therefore the amount of gain reduction.

Now that you understand this, let's take the gain of the s2s_fx_Loop_128_crude Clips down a bit. They are too loud and too compressed for my taste, and our Master output is clipping every time they play.

41. Click on the first s2s_fx_Loop_128_crude Clip starting at bar 47. [Shift-click] on the last of these Clips, occurring at 93.3.1, to select the whole range of them.
42. In Clip View, reduce the Gain of all of these Clips to –3.41 dB.

Now these Clips compress less and are not so overpowering.

Important! Conversely, a Track's Volume setting, as determined by the slider/value in the Mixer, occurs after the plug-in chain: after all the effects have done their jobs, you can set an overall volume for the Track. Adjusting this setting will not affect the Gain Reduction amount in the Compressor, because the adjustment is after the Compressor.

43. Use [shift-tab] to switch the Perc to Track View.
44. Click-and-drag in the Track's Volume box to adjust the Track Volume up or down.

The amount of gain reduction in the Compressor does not change, even when the Track Volume is at –inf dB ("negative infinity" decibels).

45. Set the Track Volume to 1.00 dB.

Hopefully, you are starting to see the interrelatedness of the various gain stages in Live. For Audio Tracks, they happen in this order:

- Clip Gain
- The Track's individual Audio Effects gain adjustments (if any) from left to right
- Track Volume
- The Master Track's Audio Effects gain adjustments (if any) from left to right
- Master Volume

Ta-da! You've made it through EQ and Compression! Feel free to apply EQs and Compressors to the Tracks that you think need them. I cannot stress enough how important these two effects will be to making your songs sound great, so spend as much time as you can with them. They are by far the two most important effects in your arsenal.

5.1.5—Using Other Audio Effects as Inserts on Tracks

If you think of EQ and Compression as salt and pepper, then the rest of Live's Audio Effects are akin to more exotic spices like coriander, turmeric, or chipotle. These effects can be used to give a particular sound a distinctive flavor.

There is no one "right" use or setting for these effects, so I won't go step-by-step through all of them as I did EQ and Compressor. However, one way you can get to know a new effect more quickly is to listen to some of its Presets to hear a range of what it is capable of. A Preset is simply a collection of settings for that Device. Remember when we used the Hot-Swap button to audition Groove templates? Let's use the same technique to preview a few Audio Effect Presets. I'll also show you how to save your own Presets and modify the default settings for a Device.

Loading and Auditioning Presets

46. In the Browser, click on the Live Device Browser button to show you Live's Instruments, MIDI Effects, and Audio Effects.
47. In the Audio Effects folder, scroll down until you find the Chorus effect in the list.

To the left of the name and icon of every Live plug-in Device, you will see a right-pointing triangle, just like the one you use to navigate folders in the Browser.

48. Click on the triangle next to the Chorus Audio Effect to open the Device and view its list of available Presets.
49. From the Preset list, click-and-drag Zorbus onto the Synth2 Track and drop it.

Live not only applies the Chorus effect to the Synth2 Track, but also applies the Zorbus Preset to the Chorus effect all in one action. Nice!

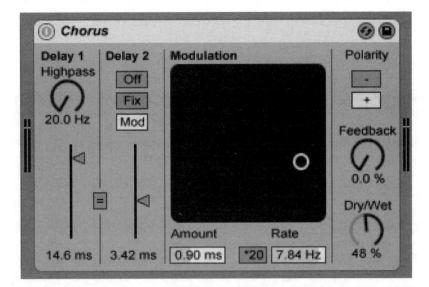

Pic. 5i: The Chorus effect with the Zorbus Preset.

50. Use the Loop Brace to Loop bars 47 through 57.
51. Solo the Synth2 Track and play the Loop.
52. Enable and disable the Chorus plug-in's Device Activator switch in the upper left of the Chorus's title bar to compare the Track with the Chorus on and off.

Pic. 5j: The Device Activator switch.

This makes the CST1 Clip seem quite a bit more interesting. But let's see what else the Chorus effect has to offer. In the upper right corner of the Chorus plug-in's title bar, you will see two buttons: the Hot-Swap Presets button and the Save Preset button.

53. With Live still playing the Loop, click on the Hot-Swap button in the title bar of the Chorus effect.

Pic. 5k: The Hot-Swap Preset and Save Preset buttons in an Audio Effect.

Live jumps the focus to the Chorus Presets in the Browser, where a new message is displayed, alerting you that you are now in Hot-Swap mode.

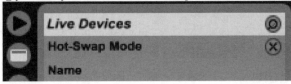

Pic. 5l: The Hot-Swap mode indicator in the Browser.

While in Hot-Swap mode, you can double-click on any of the current Effect's Presets to apply them and hear what they sound like. You can also use your [up/down arrow] keys to select a Preset, and the [enter] key to apply it:

54. Press [arrow up] to select the Yo Man! Preset, and then press [enter] to apply it.

Notice how the Chorus plug-in's settings change. Wow, that is quite a different sound! Try another one:

55. Press the [up arrow] to select another Preset, and [enter] to apply it.

Step through all the Presets. When you find the one that you like, do one of the following to exit Hot-Swap mode:

- At the top of the Browser, click on the X button to the right of the orange Hot-Swap mode message.
- In the Chorus plug-in on the Synth2 Track, click on the Hot-Swap button again.

Hot-Swap mode is disabled. Just as an experiment, do the following:

56. Double-click on another Chorus Preset (while not in Hot-Swap mode).

Live adds a second Chorus Device on the current Track with the Preset that you double-clicked on! Not what we want. To remove the second Chorus Device, do one of the following:

- Press [cmd-z/ctrl-z] or go Edit > Undo to Undo the previous action.
- Click in the Device's title bar to select it, and then press [delete].

You're back to just the one Chorus Device.

Note that you can still make changes to any Preset after applying it. Go ahead and do this. This will not alter the Preset's original settings.

Saving Presets

You will probably find some settings that you really like in various Live Devices as you work with them. If you think you will want to work with those same settings again on another Track, or even in another Live Set, consider saving your settings to the Library as a Preset.

57. In the same Chorus Device, click on the Save Preset button. You are immediately taken to the Live Device Browser, inside the Chorus Preset list again, but this time there is a new Preset icon, and the Preset's name is highlighted and ready for you to rename it. Give your new Chorus Preset a name, perhaps "CST1 Chorus." Hit [enter] when you are done.

You have saved these settings to the Library for future use. You can recall the Preset in another Chorus Device by using Hot-Swap mode or simply dragging the Preset from the Browser onto the Chorus Device you wish to apply it to. Simple.

Save as Default

A Device's default settings are usually not what you want, and sometimes you will find yourself applying the same kind of settings repeatedly, wishing that the default settings were more useful to your regular needs. Thankfully, this is easily remedied. Every plug-in has a Save as Default function.

For example: In the EQ Eight, I like to start with node 1 as a low-cut filter and node 4 as a high shelf. Let's make it so that all your EQ Eights will be this way when you load the default EQ Eight Device:

58. Double-click on the EQ Eight in the Live Device Browser to apply it to the Synth2 Track that you are currently working on. It can be before or after the Chorus—you choose.

59. Click on the low-cut filter mode button (the leftmost filter mode) to change node 1 to this shape.

60. Select node 4 by clicking on the associated number 4 on the left of the Freq, Gain, and Q dials. Change the filter mode to high shelf (fifth from the left) to set this mode for node 4.

61. [Ctrl-click/right-click] on the EQ Eight's yellow title bar and select Save as Default from the contextual menu.

Now, whenever you load an EQ Eight—not a Preset, just the Device by itself—it will start with these settings. If you want to change the default settings to something else, just repeat this process with the new settings. This works for any Live Device.

Don't forget to

62. Save your Set!

Exercise 5.2—Applying Audio Effects as a Send Effect

So far, we have only applied Audio Effects directly to Tracks in serial (one after another), in a method I described as an insert effect. Let's try the second method, parallel processing, known as a send effect.

The beauty of a send effect is that the effect can be shared among some, or all, of your Tracks in differing amounts. This saves precious CPU power, and gives the Tracks that send to this effect a similar sound. The most traditional use of a send effect is a reverb effect, which simulates the sound of reflections in an enclosed space. Let's start with that.

5.2.1—Applying a Reverb Send Effect

Do It! Let's get ready to use send effects:

- You can continue from right where you left off at the end of Exercise 5.1 and use Save As... to save the Set as My Exercise 5.2.als, or
- You can open Exercise 5.2.als from the supplied Sets in Book Content > Exercise Sets, and then perform a Save As... and save your Set as My Exercise 5.2.als.

Although you can create send effects in either View, we'll be using Arrangement View for this exercise.

Before we get can create a send effect, we must make sure that the Returns and the Mixer are visible. If you opened Exercise 5.2.als from the supplied Book Content folder, I have made sure they are already visible, but let's briefly review these commands from chapter 1 anyway:

- Make sure that Return Tracks are visible: Look for two Tracks, one named "A Return" and the other "B Return," just above the Master Track. If you do not see them, you can make them visible in one of three ways:

- Press [cmd-opt-r/ctrl-alt-r] to toggle them on and off.
- Go View > Returns.
- Enable the Show/Hide Returns button—which is an "R"—on the lower-right edge of the Arrangement window.

- Make sure that the Mixer is visible: Look for a vertical row next to your Tracks that has your Track Activator, Solo, Volume, Pan, and Send controls. If you do not see them, do one of the following:
  - Press [cmd-opt-m/ctrl-alt-m] to toggle them on and off.
  - Go View > Mixer.
  - Enable the Show/Hide Mixer button—which is an "M"—on the lower-right edge of the Arrangement window.

Okay, now you're ready.

Applying a send effect is a two-step process:

- Place the effect you want to share on a Return Track.
- Turn up the corresponding Send dial on the Tracks you want to have the effect on.

Do It! Let's give it a try:

1. In the Browser, click on the Live Device Browser button.
2. In the Audio Effects folder, scroll down to the Reverb Device.
3. Drag the Reverb Device onto the Track A Return and drop it. The Detail View switches to the Track View for the Return Track, which now has the Reverb Device on it, and the Track is renamed "A Reverb" as a result.

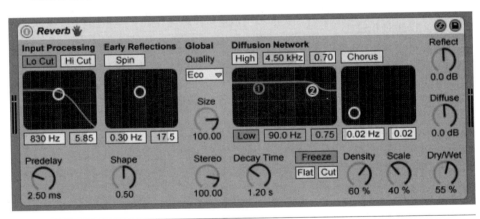

Pic. 5m: The Reverb Audio Effect.

This is the destination that all of your "Sends" will "Return" to.

4. Find the Send A level in the Mixer for the Perc Track. Click-and-drag its value up to –20 dB. (You can see an exact value down in the Status Bar at the very bottom of the Live's interface as you change the Send level.)

Pic. 5n: The Send A level box for a Track in Arrangement View.

Pic. 5o: The Status Bar showing an exact value for the Send A level box.

5. In a similar fashion, set the Send A level on the One Shots Track to –6 dB.
6. Set the Send A level on the Synth2 Track to –10 dB.
7. Play back the arrangement.

You should hear reverb on the Perc, One Shots, and Synth2 Tracks. Solo these Tracks if you want to hear them in isolation. You will hear a different amount of reverb on each of these three Tracks, because you are sending different amounts of each Track to the Return Track with the Reverb on it. Remember that each Track's Send control is sending a copy of that Track's sound to the corresponding Return Track (where it gets reverberated, in this case), and that the Send value controls the amount that is being sent from each Track. Since there is a Reverb on the A Return Track, you can think of each Track's Send value as controlling "reverb amount" for that Track.

Of course, you can still modify the Reverb's settings or choose a Preset:

8. Double-click on the A Reverb Return Track to show its Track View and the Reverb Device.
9. Click on the Reverb's Hot-Swap button.
10. In the Reverb Device's Preset list, open the Hall folder and double-click on the Large Hall Preset to apply it. Play the arrangement to hear the difference.

Important! When using an effect as a send effect in this way, it is traditional to set the effect's Wet/Dry value to 100% wet, or "all effect, no dry signal." This is because you already have a "dry" version of the signal passing through the Track to the Master, so the copy that is sent to the Return Track should be 100% effect. If you set the Return Track effect to less than 100%, you would be sending a second dry version of the Track to the Master, which will only cause problems when mixing. Note that the Large Hall Preset has the Wet/Dry dial up at 100%. This Preset was intended to be used on a Return Track in this fashion.

5.2.2—Applying a Delay Send Effect

Send effects are a little more advanced than are insert effects, so repetition is good practice. Let's add a Ping Pong Delay effect on our B Return and send some signal to it with a few of our Track's Send B values. Also, let's try doing this exercise in Session View to see the differences.

11. Switch to Session View.

12. Make sure that your Mixer, Sends and Return Tracks are all showing. (Check the View menu if you are unsure.)

13. In the Live Device Browser list's Audio Effects folder, scroll down until you see Ping Pong Delay. Drag this Device onto the B Return Track and drop it.

Pic. 5p: The Ping Pong Delay Audio Effect.

14. Turn the Dry/Wet dial all the way up to 100%.

15. Set the Feedback to 40%.

16. Change the Center Frequency to 2.29 kHz.

17. Set the Beat Division to 2.

Now let's send it some signal from our Tracks. In Session View, you are given Send level dials instead of numbers. As you rotate a Send dial, the Status Bar displays the exact value.

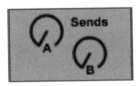

Pic. 5q: The Mixer's Send dials in Session View.

18. On the Perc Track, turn up Send B to –20 dB.

19. On the One Shots Track, turn up Send B to –14 dB.

20. On the Synth2 Track, turn up Send B to –6 dB.

21. Play the arrangement from the beginning.

Important! Pressing play in Session View still plays the arrangement you have been working on in Arrangement View unless you also start launching Clips in the Clip grid.

The Ping Pong Delay is delaying only a narrow range of the frequencies it is being sent (which are centered around 2.29 kHz), which is in the upper midrange. This helps to keep it from getting muddy in the bass, and adds a little bit of shimmer on each of your sending Tracks.

Try varying the Send A and Send B amounts while the arrangement plays to hear the effect, and then choose your own Send levels.

So now you have been through the two primary ways of applying Audio Effects: using Track insert effects and send effects. Both have their many uses. Don't be afraid to experiment—you won't break anything! Live's effects are so plentiful, flexible, and easy to use that they should provide endless new horizons for your music.

You'll notice that we did not yet cover putting Audio Effects on the Master Track. Not to worry: I'm saving that for the next section, when we talk about Audio Effect Racks.

22. Save your Set by pressing [cmd-s/ctrl-s].

Exercise 5.3—Audio Effect Racks

There are four types of Racks in Ableton Live: Audio Effect Racks, MIDI Effect Racks, Instrument Racks, and Drum Racks. I like to call Racks "rabbit hole" Devices, because once you start to explore them, they are truly endless in their possibilities. I have yet to think up a routing that cannot be solved with some combination of Racks, and I have spent long days and nights in the studio trying!

Audio Effect Racks are a unique feature of Ableton Live. They allow you to combine all manner of serial and parallel processing on a single Track in ways never before possible. But best of all, they give you a way to gang multiple processing variables together onto eight Macro dials, which allow you to play your effects like a music instrument.

Here are some of the more obvious benefits of using Racks:

- Racks can simplify complex multi-effect processing tasks—such as Master Track processing—into eight streamlined dials.
- Racks can create a signature sound-design transform that can completely reshape a sound with the twist of a single dial.
- Racks can greatly simplify your live or DJ effects setup so that only the controls you want to tweak are showing.
- Racks can save you time by allowing you to save your regularly used Audio Effect Chains as a Preset for quick recall.

Once you become more familiar with what an Audio Effect Rack is capable of, you will likely begin to think up your own Rack recipes to manifest your sound-shaping visions! And just like a chef in training, you should sample great food from around the world to broaden your imagination and inspire new culinary creations! Rather than trying to further explain what Racks are capable of, we're going to try a few of the included Preset Racks before we make our own.

Live includes a sizeable library of Audio Effect Rack Presets for you to try out, and they come sorted into a variety of applications. Some are intended for individual Tracks, some for Return Tracks, and some for the Master Track. Some Racks are subtle in what they do and some are anything but! For maximum impact, I am going to have you try out these Racks on the Master Track, where the Rack's effects will affect the entire mix so you can plainly hear what they do.

5.3.1—Audio Effect Rack Presets

Do It! It's time to explore the wondrous world of Audio Effect Racks:

- You can continue from right where you left off at the end of Exercise 5.2 and use Save As... to save the Set as My Exercise 5.3.als, or
- You can open Exercise 5.3.als from the supplied Sets in Book Content > Exercise Sets, and then perform a Save As... and save your Set as My Exercise 5.3.als.

Let's audition a series of Racks on the Master Track.

1. Double-click on the Master Track's Track name to bring up the Master Track's Track View, which shows that the Track is empty of any Devices.
2. In the Browser, click on the Live Device Browser button to bring up the list of Live Devices.
3. Open the Audio Effects folder; the first Device in the list is Audio Effect Rack. Click on the triangle to the left of the Device to show its list of Presets.

Notice that the Audio Effect Rack Presets are subdivided into folders to group them by application. There are Preset groups for basses, guitars, drums and vocals, and also for reverb, rhythmic, and mastering. Try these out in your spare time. They will give you a big insight into what Live's effects are capable of and will jump-start your understanding of them.

4. Open the Performance & DJ folder. Scroll down to Cut-o-matic. Double-click on this Preset to add it to your Master Track.

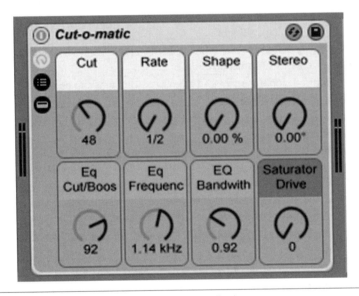

Pic. 5r: The Cut-o-matic Audio Effect Rack Preset on the Master Track.

This Preset is not overly extreme and will be fairly easy to understand and listen to. All Racks consist of eight Macro dials with names. Adjust each of these dials to see what they do. The dial colors indicate that the top row of dials all adjust parameters that are related, while the lower row of dial colors suggest two different types of transforms. Take some time to explore some of the various combinations that can be achieved with just these eight knobs.

When you are ready,

5. Click on the Show/Hide Devices button on the left of the Rack.

Pic. 5s: The Show/Hide Devices button on a Rack.

This button "opens" the Rack so that you can begin to see what is going on "under the hood." You will see that this Rack contains four effects: an Auto Pan, an EQ Eight, a Saturator, and a Limiter.

6. Double-click on the EQ Eight's title bar to unfold it.

Cool! All Live Devices can be folded and unfolded by double-clicking on their title bar or by pressing the [+] or [–] keys when it is selected. This helps save space when you have very long chains of effects.

Now that you can see the EQ Eight, go back to the Rack controls and adjust the three orange dials on the second row and watch what they do. Essentially, the three lower dials work with the EQ Eight's nodes 2 and 3 simultaneously, modifying the Frequency, Gain, and Q dials, respectively.

7. Double-click on the Auto Pan Device to unfold it.
8. Adjust the first dial, Cut, and notice what it does in the Auto Pan and EQ Eight.

This Macro dial adjusts parameters in two Devices at once. Interesting! You can combine controls on multiple Devices to create complex sonic adjustments. This is the real power of Audio Effect Racks.

Feel free to explore all the dials and their relationships to the Rack's Devices.

When you have learned all you can from this Rack,

9. Click on the Hot-Swap button on the Rack's title bar.

Load another Audio Effect Rack Preset and see what it has to offer. Open it up and see how it works. Try Presets from several of the folders. Take a survey of the vast possibilities of Audio Effect Racks.

And when you are done,

10. Delete the Rack from the Master Track by clicking on its name in the title bar and pressing [delete].

Now, let's make one of our own.

5.3.2—Creating a Basic Multi-Effects Rack

You may have noticed that we have not yet attempted to improve or manipulate the sound of your Synth1 Track, and it could definitely use some help. That is because I've got something special planned for this Track to help it really stand out.

Keep in mind that Racks are definitely an intermediate- to advanced-level concept. If this section seems a bit harder than everything else so far, that's because it is. Stay focused and dive in.

11. Begin by switching to Arrangement View, and Looping bars 27 through 57.

12. Solo the Synth1 Track, and then double-click on the Track name to bring up its Track View, which is currently empty.

13. In the Live Device Browser, inside the Audio Effects folder, find a Device called Audio Effect Rack. Double-click on it to place it on the Synth1 Track.

Not very interesting, right? That is because an Audio Effect Rack by itself does not do anything—it is simply a container for placing combinations of effects. See where it says "Drop Audio Effects Here"? Let's do that!

14. In the Audio Effects list, find Auto Filter. Click on the expander triangle next to it to show its list of Presets. Drag the first Preset, Cut-O-Move H, from the Browser and drop it in the empty Audio Effect Rack where it says to do so.

Note that the Rack "bookends" the Auto Filter. This effect is contained within the Audio Effect Rack. That doesn't mean much now, but it will. Let's add a few more effects:

15. In the Audio Effects list, find Chorus. Click on the expander triangle next to it to show its list of Presets. Drag the Preset Resorus from the Browser and hover it over the Track View area, but do not drop it yet.

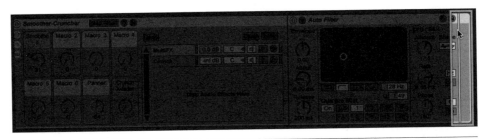

Pic. 5t: Dropping a second effect after the first, but still within the Rack.

As you drag this second effect over the Track View area, you will see a vertical yellow line appear near your cursor, before or after the different Devices there. You saw this before when placing the second Audio Effect on the Perc Track. This line is telling you where the Chorus will be inserted if you let go of it there. Currently, there are four possible places you could drop it:

- Far left: Before the Audio Effect Rack entirely.
- Second from the left: Inside the Rack and before the Auto Filter.
- Third from the left: Inside the Rack and after the Auto Filter.
- Far right: After the Audio Effect Rack entirely.

Drop the Chorus at the third location: inside the Rack and after the Auto Filter. It should look like this:

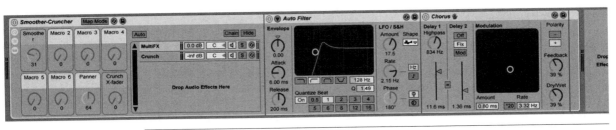

Pic. 5u: The Auto Filter and the Chorus both inside the Audio Effect Rack.

Continue to add the remaining effects in a similar fashion, dropping them after the previous effect, but still inside the Rack:

16. In the Audio Effects list, find Simple Delay. Click on the expander triangle next to it to show its list of Presets. Drag the Preset Dotted Eighth Note from the Browser and drop it in the Audio Effect Rack after the Chorus.

17. In the Audio Effects list, find Reverb. Click on the expander triangle next to it to show its list of Presets. Open the subfolder, Special, and scroll to the bottom. Drag the Preset Wide Ambience from the Browser and drop it in the empty Audio Effect Rack after the Simple Delay.

18. In the Audio Effects list, find Compressor. Click on the expander triangle next to it to show its list of Presets. Drag the Preset Gentle Squeeze from the Browser and drop it in the Audio Effect Rack after the Reverb.

Sounds cool, but so far none of what we have done is any different from simply dropping these four effects on the Track in a row without the Rack: the audio from the Track goes through the effects in a serial fashion, and we hear the result of these effects in the mix. Let's make it more interesting.

On the far left edge of the Rack you will see three buttons, the bottom of which is lit.

Pic. 5v: The Audio Effect Rack's three Show/Hide buttons.

- Show/Hide Macro Controls—Enable this button. Eight Macro dials appear. These dials are for attaching your favorite effects controls to for easy access.
- Show/Hide Chain List—Enable this button. The Chain list shows the available Chains for this Rack. Chains are parallel to each other, and can contain Audio Effect Devices.
- Show/Hide Devices—Disable and reenable this button: this button will show or hide the list of Audio Effect Devices on one of the Chains in the previous Chain list.

All three buttons should now be enabled, and you can now see all three sections of the Audio Effect Rack: Macro dials, the Chain list, and Devices. Let's get more familiar with these areas.

5.3.3—Serial and Parallel Processing with the Chain List

Chains are one of those features that are more easily shown than described. Walk through the next few steps, and the definition of what a Chain is will emerge.

Currently, your Audio Effect Rack has a single Chain and it is named, not surprisingly, "Chain."

Pic. 5w: The Audio Effect Rack Chain named "Chain."

Let's begin by renaming it:

19. Do one of the following to rename Chain to "MultiFX":
- Click on the name "Chain" to select it, and then press [cmd-r/ctrl-r].
- [Ctrl-click/right-click] on Chain and select Rename from the contextual menu.
- Click on the name "Chain" to select it, and go Edit > Rename.
   Now let's create a second Chain:
20. In the Audio Effect Device list, find Saturator. Click on the expander triangle next to it to show its list of Presets. Drag the Preset Hot Tubes from the Browser and drop it in the Chain list area where it says "Drop Audio Effects Here."
21. In the Saturator, click on the Soft Clip button to turn it on.
   A second Chain appears named, once again, as "Chain."
22. Rename this second Chain as "Crunch," using one of the methods above.
23. In the Audio Effects list, find Redux. Click on the expander triangle next to it to show its list of Presets. Drag the Preset Mirage from the Browser and drop it after the Saturator, but still within the Rack.
24. Adjust the Downsample dial on the Redux to 10.

You now have two Chains: MultiFX and Crunch. Click on the name of the MultiFX Chain and you will see the effects on that Chain. Click on the Crunch Chain and you will see the effects on that Chain. These two Chains exist side by side, or "in parallel." This is much the same as having effects inserted on a Track in series, and then having a Return Track with different effects on it.

Okay, definition time: A Chain is a series of Audio Effect Devices within an Audio Effect Rack. You can have an unlimited number of Chains in a Rack. The Track's audio passes into the Rack, where it splits and is processed by all of the Chains of effects simultaneously, and then is mixed back together at the end of the Rack.

Audio Effects Racks Signal Flow

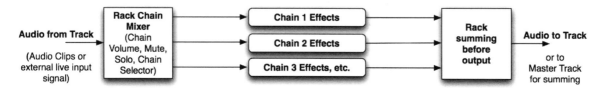

Pic. 5x: Signal diagram of an Audio Effect Rack.

If there are Devices after the Rack, they are the next recipients of that Track's audio, and then it flows to the Mixer section, to the Master Track, and out to your speakers.

In the Chain list, to the right of the Chain name, there are five icons. They are as follows:

- Chain Volume—This volume slider controls the amount of signal that goes through this Chain.
- Chain Pan—This panner positions the Chain in the stereo field.
- Chain Activator—Enables or disables (mutes) the Chain.
- Chain Solo—Solos the Chains one at a time.
- Chain Hot-Swap—Allows you to swap out the entire Chain with another Chain Preset.

Let's isolate each Chain so that you can hear their effect on the audio individually:

25. Click on the Chain Solo button on the MultiFX Chain.
26. Play the Looped bars of the arrangement.

    You hear the first Chain we made.
27. Disable the Chain Solo button on the MultiFX Chain.
28. Click on the Chain Solo button on the Crunch Chain.

    You hear the second Chain we made.
29. Disable the Chain Solo button on the Crunch Chain.

You hear both Chains happening simultaneously, or in parallel.

Voilá: serial and parallel processing all on one Track, made possible by an Audio Effect Rack. Make sense?

But wait: It gets better!

5.3.4—Audio Effect Rack Macro Dials

When I was a kid, I had an electric guitar and several effects pedals. I remember vividly, even then, wishing I could have at least ten arms so I could be playing the guitar and tweaking all the effects pedal knobs at the same time.

Presently, we have five Audio Effects on one Chain and two on another. Collectively, there must be several dozen different parameters that we could tweak on those effects. And because they are on different Chains, it's inconvenient to get to the parameters quickly. Macro dials will not give you ten arms, but they will provide a way to easily and simultaneously adjust a bunch of parameters that we want to have easy access to.

Assigning a parameter to a Macro dial is a simple five-step process:

· Click on the Map Mode button to enter Macro Map Mode.
· Click on the parameter on one of the Devices in one of your Chains that you wish to assign to a Macro dial.
· Click on a Map button underneath the Macro dial you want to assign it to.
· Optionally, adjust the range of values you would like the dial to send in the Mapping Browser.
· Click on the Map Mode button to exit Macro Map Mode.

Let's assign some of your favorite controls to the Macro dials. Then you will see just how powerful Audio Effect Racks are.

30. On the Synth1 Track, in the Audio Effect Rack Chain list, solo the MultiFX Chain.
31. Click on the Map Mode button in the title bar of the Audio Effect Rack that we have made.

Pic. 5y: The Map Mode button in an Audio Effect Rack.

A lot of things just happened:

· Many controls on in the Rack turned green. Green indicates which controls can be mapped to a Macro dial.
· Map buttons appeared underneath each of the Macro dials. This is how you choose which dial you want to assign a control to.
· An area called the Mapping Browser replaced the File/Device Browser. This is where you edit the range of values that a Macro dial will send.

While in Macro Map Mode, you should not attempt to do anything besides assigning effects parameters to Macro dials; otherwise, you may experience some unexpected results.

32. Click on the MultiFX Chain name to show that Chain's Devices.
33. Now click on the Auto Filter's Filter Cutoff parameter below the filter graph—it currently reads 1.14 kHz. When you do, a small black box surrounds it to show that it is selected.
34. Now click on the Map button beneath Macro 1 to assign Filter Cutoff to that Macro dial. The name of that dial is now Frequency.
35. Click on Map Mode to exit Macro Map Mode.

The screen returns to normal.

Play the Looped section again and adjust the new Frequency Macro dial. Cool—but no different from adjusting the same parameter in the Auto Filter. Let's add another parameter to the same dial:

36. Enter Macro Map Mode.
37. Click on the Q control just below Filter Cutoff. It currently reads 1.76.
38. Map it also to Macro 1 (currently called Frequency) by pressing the same Map button under the dial as before.

Without exiting Map Mode, adjust the Macro 1 dial (which has been renamed back to Macro 1, now that more than one parameter is assigned to it). As you move it, both Filter Cutoff and Q are adjusted!

Notice that a new entry appears in the Mapping Browser up above. Let's explore that.

The Mapping Browser has two entries, one for each control that we have mapped so far. Each entry lists which Macro dial is assigned to which Device and which control. And on the far right are two columns: Min and Max.

Min and Max control the minimum and maximum values you want to adjust between. Or, thought of another way, they set the values that turning the dial full left and full right will achieve for that mapped control. The default is that the Macro dial will control the parameter's entire range of motion. But that is not always exactly what you want.

Presently, the Filter Cutoff ranges from 25 Hz to 19.9 kHz. When the low-cut filter is up all the way, it removes so much of the sound that there is nothing much useful left. Let's fix that:

39. Click on the Max box for Filter Cutoff to highlight it. Type in 10000, which sets a value of 10 kHz. Press [enter] to commit to the value.

Now when you turn the dial all the way to the right, the topmost value achievable is 10 kHz.

Similarly, it would be nice if the Q did not disappear so drastically when the knob is turned left.

40. Click on the Min value for the Q entry and drag it up to 1.00.

The Q starts 60% of the way up the scale and increases to 100%. Better.

Just to show you the power of these Macro dials, I am going to map another ten parameters onto this same dial so it will be controlling a dozen parameters at once. Entering this much data may seem cumbersome, but there is a sizeable sound-shaping reward for you once you are done. Be sure to play the Loop and turn the Macro 1 dial periodically while mapping these parameters if you want to hear the complexity evolve. Ready?

41. While still in Map Mode, click on LFO Amount in the Auto Filter, and map it to Macro 1. Set the Min to 15 and the Max to 25.
42. In the Chorus, map Delay 1 Time to the same knob.

Yes, you can map controls from multiple Devices to the same knob!

43. In the Mapping Browser, [ctrl-click/right-click] on the entry for Delay 1 Time and choose Invert Range.

The Min and Max values swap places. You can set a high value to the left end of the dial and a low value to the right end. Nice!

44. In the Chorus, also map Delay 2 Time. Do not modify the Min/Max values.
45. Also in the Chorus, map Dry/Wet. Min: 30%. Max: 70%.
46. In the Simple Delay, map Feedback and Dry/Wet to Macro 1 as well (one at a time). Feedback: Min: 20%. Max: 70%. Dry/Wet: Min: 15%. Max: 55%.
47. In the Reverb, map Stereo Image and Dry/Wet to the same Macro 1 dial. Stereo Image: Min: 20.00. Max: 120.00. Dry/Wet: Min: 30%. Max: 60%.
48. Finally, in the Compressor, map Threshold to Macro 1. Min: –28.0 dB Max: –38.0 dB.
49. Exit Map Mode, and try your creation.

So you can see now how powerful a single Macro dial can be! And there are eight of them—just imagine the possibilities!

Remember that the MultiFX Chain is soloed—we haven't even dealt with the second Chain yet. Let's do a few more (much simpler!) mappings to other knobs to finish this Rack off.

50. Unsolo the MultiFX Chain so that both Chains are audible.
51. Enter Map mode again.
52. Click on the Chain Volume box for the MultiFX Chain in the Chain list, which currently reads 0.00 dB. Map this to the Macro 8 dial. Min: 0.00 dB. Max: –inf dB.
53. Click on the Chain Volume box for the Crunch Chain in the Chain list, which also currently reads 0.00 dB. Map this to the Macro 8 dial as well. Min: –inf dB. Max: 0.00 dB.
54. In the Crunch Chain on the Redux Device, map the Downsample dial to Macro 8. Min: 0. Max: 45.
55. In the Saturator, map Drive to Macro 8. Min: 36.0 dB. Max: 4.5 dB.

Turn Macro 8 (now called Chain Volume) while the Loop plays. You now have a crossfader between your two Chains, and the distortion increases as you crossfade.

56. Map the Chain Pan controls for both Chains to Macro 7.

One dial pans both effects Chains. The possibilities are endless!

5.3.5—Renaming Dials and Saving your Rack Creation

Let's rename our Macro dials so we don't forget what they are. Do one of the following:

- Click once on the Macro 1 dial. The black brackets tell you that it is selected. Press [cmd-r/ctrl-r] to rename the dial.
- Click once on the Macro 1 dial. The black brackets tell you that it is selected. Go Edit > Rename to rename the dial.
- [Ctrl-click/right-click] on the dial and choose Rename from the contextual menu.

57. Rename dial 1 "Smoother" or something equally descriptive.

58. Rename dial 7 "Panner" or something equally descriptive.
59. Rename dial 8 "Crunch X-fader" or something equally descriptive.
    You can also color the dials if that helps you remember what they do.
60. [Ctrl-click/right-click] on the Smoother dial 1. Choose a bluish color from the available color squares in the contextual menu.
61. [Ctrl-click/right-click] on the Panner dial 7. Choose a yellow color from the available color squares in the contextual menu.
62. [Ctrl-click/right-click] on the Crunch X-fader dial 8. Choose a red/orange color from the available color squares in the contextual menu.

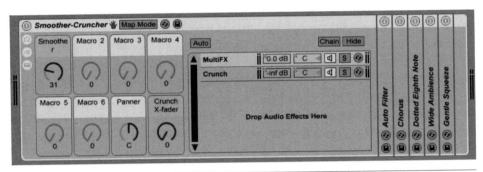

Pic. 5z: The finished Smoother Cruncher Audio Effect Rack Device.

Finally, do the following:

63. Disable the Show/Hide Devices button and the Show/Hide Chain List button so that you are looking at just the Macro dials.

There you have it—a compact, easy-to-use Rack for transforming your sounds in one particular way.

Best of all, you can save your Rack creations to the Library for future use in other Projects:

64. Click on the Save Preset button in the Rack's title bar.

Live jumps you to the Device Browser inside of Audio Effect Racks and prompts you for a name.

65. Save your Rack as "Smoother-Cruncher" or something equally descriptive.
    And finally, don't forget:
66. Save your Set by pressing [cmd-s/ctrl-s]!

Third-party Effects

In addition to the wide array of effects that come with Live, you can customize your sound-shaping possibilities by adding third-party effects created by other companies. Just the way that every guitar or keyboard or microphone has its own unique sound characteristics, so a third-party EQ or compressor plug-in does its job in a unique way and offers a unique coloration. Live supports Steinberg's Virtual Studio Technology (VST) and Apple's Audio Units (AU) formats (Mac only). Any plug-in in either of these formats will work with Live, and most will allow you to map their controls in Racks and automate their parameters. Most third-party effects offer a free trial or demo period wherein you can try their plug-in for free to see if you like it. Additionally, there are hundreds, maybe thousands, of freeware and shareware plug-ins available online. Try searching in your browser for "freeware VST effects" or "shareware AU effects" to find some of the many sites that distribute these.

Cool! I've gotten permission to distribute installers for several of my favorite third-party effects and Instruments. You will find the installers and instructions in the Book Content Install folder that you downloaded, and a description of these plug-ins in appendix F. Some of them are freeware, so you can use them indefinitely, and others are demo versions that will expire after a trial period. If you try a demo version and like it, I highly encourage you to pick it up from the vendor's website. I chose these particular plug-ins because they will add a unique sonic flavor to your toolbox and because they are some of the best I have found at what they do.

Summary

- Generally speaking, there are two ways to use Audio Effects: in serial as an insert effect, or in parallel as a send effect.
- Live's Audio Effects can be found in the Live Device Browser in the Audio Effects folder, and can be applied to any Track by dragging and dropping it from the Browser onto the Track or by double-clicking on the Device in the Browser to add it to the currently selected Track.
- Live's EQ Three and EQ Eight are used for making tonal adjustments.
- Live's Compressor is used for making dynamic range reductions.
- All of Live's Devices have a selection of Presets, which can be browsed and hot-swapped. As well, a Device's settings can be saved as a Preset into the Live Library for use in future Sets, or saved as the default state.
- An Audio Effect placed on a Return Track can be accessed from any Track for processing with the Track's corresponding Send dial.
- Audio Effect Racks offer unique serial and parallel processing combinations, as well as Macro dial assignments for easy manipulation of multiple parameters at once. Racks can also be saved as Presets.
- Live is capable of running VST and AU third-party effects and Instrument plug-ins, which greatly expands Live's already formidable processing possibilities.

Chapter 6

RECORDING AUDIO WITH LIVE

Thus far we have managed to create our song from prerecorded Loops, samples, and Presets. It is much easier to learn the mechanics of a new program without the additional challenges of having to be creative on demand and manage performance anxiety. But now that you have a majority of the program's features under your belt, you will no doubt be eager to make your own recordings and samples to put your own unique stamp on your sound. Understanding all of the previous lessons up to this point will allow you to take on the additional technical and musical challenges of making your own recordings with more confidence.

Setting Up for Recording

If you are interested in making recordings with Live, I am going to assume that you have an external audio interface (connected via FireWire, USB, or PCMCIA) and that it was connected and powered on before you booted your computer and launched Live. Before you record digital audio, you should make sure that your audio interface is configured correctly for working with Live. Chapter 8, "Best Practices," looks closely at Live's Audio Preferences and discusses methods for tuning your audio interface and system settings. As well, if you are new to audio, digital audio, or computers in general, you will want to read the various appendices on those topics, because this section may use some terminology you are unfamiliar with.

Once you have Live's Preferences and your audio interface configured properly, its time to have a look at the In/Out section of Live's Audio Tracks.

The In/Out Section

Make sure that the In/Out section is visible, using [cmd-opt-i/ctrl-alt-i] to show/hide it. You'll make your first recording in Session View, so let's start there, although the In/Out section is exactly the same in either View.

Pic. 6a: The In/Out section of an Audio Track.

The top two pull-downs control the Audio From options, while the bottom two control the Audio To options. This simple interface will allow for some fairly sophisticated routing options in addition to allowing recording external sources through your audio interface. The middle three buttons are for selecting monitoring options, which we'll cover last.

Audio From Input Types and Input Channels

Here are the likely input types and their respective input channel options, if any:

- Ext. (External) In—Select External In if you want to record an external audio signal (guitar, bass, keyboard, microphone, and so on) in through your audio interface. Input channel options are taken directly from your selections on the Preferences > Audio > Input Config page, and will consist of the various mono and stereo input channels available on your audio interface.
- Configure—This is not an input type so much as a handy shortcut directly to Live's audio interface input channel configuration Preferences for enabling or disabling inputs on your audio interface for use with the External In input type.
- Reason—If you have Propellerhead Reason, or another ReWire slave program installed and running, you can select it as an input type here. When Reason is selected, the Input Channels submenu will consist of Reason's 64 Audio Interface outputs in mono or stereo options.
- Resampling—Another genius Live feature: When you choose this option, anything playing through your main outputs is additionally routed to the input of your selected Track for recording. Want to bounce eight Tracks of backing vocals or drums to a single stereo pair? Solo the Tracks you want to bounce (or mute the ones you don't want to bounce), select Resampling as the input type, arm for recording, and press record. Does it get any easier? There are no input channel options with Resampling, since the function is hardwired to the Master outputs.
- (Track name)—You might be surprised to see the name of every other Track in your Set listed here as an input type option. Similar to Resampling, you can record the audio from any other Track in your Set. Perhaps you have some amazingly complex audio effects processing on a Track that you want to bounce to an audio file. Or perhaps you have a MIDI Instrument that sounds perfect but is taking up too many resources. You could select it as an input and record it to an Audio Track and then delete the Instrument to free up resources. Input channel options for individual Track input types are often many and varied here:
- If the input Track is an Audio Track, you will be presented with three options:
- Pre FX—The input is taken from the selected Track at a point in the signal chain before any Audio Effects on that Track, which is also before the Mixer.
- Post FX—The input is taken from the selected Track at a point after any Audio Effects on the Track, but before the Mixer section.

- Post Mixer—The input is taken from the selected Track at a point after any Audio Effects and after the Mixer, which includes any Track Panning and Track Volume settings/automation.
- If the input is an Audio Track with an Audio Effect Rack, or a MIDI Track with an Instrument, Instrument Rack, or a Drum Rack, you will be presented with the above three options, plus a potentially very long list of signal access points. For example, if you select the Impulse Track as in input source, the input channels include an output from each of the eight sample Slots so you could record any one drum's output to a new Audio Clip. In the case of a Drum Rack input type, you are presented with Pre FX, Post FX, and Post Mixer options for every drum pad and Rack Return in your Drum Rack—a very long list indeed!

Audio To Output Types and Output Channels

Output type and output channel selection is similar to input type and channel selection. Here are the available output types and output channel options if any:

- Ext. Out—Select External Out if you would like to divert the Track's output to a different audio interface output than the one assigned to your Master output. You might do this to process the Track externally with a hardware processor, to send the Track's signal to surround speakers, or to output your various Tracks to be mixed in analog on an external mixer. External output channel options are taken directly from the Perferences > Audio > Output Config dialog box, and will consist of the mono and stereo audio interface channel options you select there.
- Configure—Again, this is not an output type so much as a handy shortcut directly to Live's audio output channel configuration Preferences for enabling or disabling outputs on your audio interface for use with the External Out output type.
- (Track Name)—Here again you will see a list of the various Audio Tracks in your Set, starting with the default output type, Master.
  - Tracks set to Master will be summed at the Master Track for output to your audio interface.
  - Tracks set to output to another Audio Track in your Set will not be sent to the Master directly, but instead will be sent to the specified Audio Track. Setting multiple Tracks to output to the same Audio Track allows for subgrouping of Tracks by setting the destination Track's Monitor to In, or bouncing Tracks to a new Audio Clip by recording the sum of Track outputs on the destination Track.
- Sends Only—This final option mutes the Track's main output, but leaves the Track's Sends enabled. This allows you to use the Return Tracks as a subgroup or to hear a Track only after it has been through a Return Track's effects. One creative use of this feature is for working in surround: make a Return Track for every speaker in your surround setup, put all your Tracks into Sends Only output, and use the Send dials to direct a particular Track to a particular Return/speaker.

Monitor

The Monitor section allows you choose between hearing the Track's input, output, or neither. Whenever a Track is monitoring an incoming signal, a small microphone icon appears in the Track Status Display.

Note that the Monitor controls are visible only when you have selected an input type other than No Input.

- In—When the Monitor is set to In, the Track will always relay the incoming signal (set in the Input Type/Channel section) and never relay audio played from a Clip in the Track. Here are some scenarios in which you might set the Track's Monitor control to In:
  - If you have several other Tracks outputting to this Track and you want hear the sum of those Tracks here.
  - If you want to have a persistent live input into Live, such as a microphone or other external instrument.
  - If you are sending MIDI to an external MIDI sound source and want to hear the audio output of the Device returned through Live.
- Auto—The Auto setting is the default, and likely the one you will use the most, because it is the most adaptable setting. It is great for punching in/out on the timeline in Arrangement View as well (covered in a following section).
  - When the Track is playing back Clips, the Track defaults to monitoring the Clips playing on the Track.
  - If no Clip is playing, or as soon as Track recording begins, the Track will monitor the incoming input signal set up in the Input Type/Channel section.
  - As well, if Live's transport is stopped, armed Tracks set to Auto Monitor mode will switch to input monitoring so you can set levels, practice a part before recording, and so on.
- Off—In this monitor mode, no audio from the Track (either from the input or Clips on the Track) will be heard, regardless of Live's recording status. Here are some scenarios of when you might want to use the Monitor Off setting:
  - If you are using external or hardware monitoring, so that you do not hear an echo of your input signal through Live.
  - If you are recording input from another Track that is also playing back through the Master, so that you do not hear it twice.
  - If you are recording something that requires no monitoring through Live, such as a speech or an all-acoustic performance.

Recording in Session View

Recording in Session View into Clip Slots is fun and easy, and Live boasts a unique work flow in which you can alternate between playback, recording, and playback again without ever needing to stop the music. You can start with a basic Loop, press play, pick up an instrument, overlay some takes, add new Loops for a new section, build an arrangement of Clips, add some more recorded takes, make effects and mix decisions . . . essentially complete an entire song without ever pressing the Stop button.

The process for making an Audio (or MIDI) Track recording in Session View can be summarized in this way:

1. Arm a Track (or Tracks) for recording.
2. Select the desired input type, input channel, and Monitoring mode in the In/Out section.
3. Check incoming audio levels and adjust accordingly.
4. If you have a backing Clip or Scene that you want to play along with while you record, launch it. Alternately, enable the metronome in the Control Bar to play along to a click at the current tempo.
5. Choose a Clip Slot for recording and click on its Clip Record button to begin recording at the next Global Quantize value.
6. When you are done—or almost done—do one of the following:

- Click on the Clip Record button again to switch from recording to playback of your new Clip at the next Global Quantize value.
- Click on another Clip Record button in a new empty Clip Slot to stop the current Clip recording and switch to a new Clip recording at the next Global Quantize value.
- Click on the Track's Clip Stop button to stop your Clip's recording at the next Global Quantize value, but continue playback of other already launched Clips.
- Click on the Stop All Clips button to stop recording and stop playback of all other currently playing Clips at the next Global Quantize value, but not stop global playback of the Arrangement Position.
- Click on the Stop button in the Control Bar to immediately stop recording and playback of all Clips and to stop global playback of the Arrangement Position.

Global Quantize and Audio Recording in Session View

The key to successful Session View Clip recording is the Global Quantize setting in the Control Bar. Just as Global Quantize affects the timing of launched Clips for synchronized playback, so too it affects the start and stop timing of recordings for Audio and MIDI Clips in Session View. It takes some practice to get the hang of it, but once you know what to expect, achieving good results should be easy.

Helpful Hints for Recording in Session View

- If you need a count-in before recording starts, you can set one at Preferences > Record Warp Launch > Count-In. When you enable this, Live will give you a metronome count-in before recording (and playback of other Clips when recording) begins. Unfortunately, you have to come back here to change the value, or to turn it off, but it works. I would much prefer this setting to be in the Control Bar where it could be quickly changed, but generally I find a setting of two bars to be what I need most of the time.
- Unlike MIDI Clips, which can be created at the length you want and then recorded into, you cannot predefine how long your Audio Clip recording will be before you click on record. This can create a challenge when you are engineering your own recordings: How do you click on something to stop recording when you are simultaneously shredding a solo on your guitar? Sure you could finish playing and go back and trim your recordings by hand, but this gets old quickly. Here are two techniques that allow you to stop recording without using your hands:
- Set the Global Quantize value to the length of the Clip you intend to record, and when you go to record, instead of clicking on the Clip Record button once, click on it twice. This will start the Clip recording and stop the recording after the selected Global Quantize value with one action, effectively recording for a specific length. Of course, if you need a value other than 1, 2, 4, or 8 bars, this technique will not work.
- If you own a MIDI footpedal (a sustain pedal works well), you can map it to control a Clip Record/Stop button so you can use your feet to do what your hands cannot.
- By default, launching a Scene will not initiate recording on an armed Audio Track, but there is a toggle switch for changing that behavior on the Preferences > Record Warp Launch page at the very bottom. If you have this enabled and you map a footpedal to the Scene Launch button (which is revealed only when you enter MIDI Map mode in Session View), you can trigger a new Scene or Clip recording with your footpedal. Use this to step through all of your Scenes, recording Clips as you go through your whole song. Alternately, set up a series of duplicate Scenes and record multiple takes to each of the Scenes by stepping on the footpedal. When you are done, delete the Clip takes you don't like.

- Perhaps the technique that requires the least amount of preparation or coordination to pull off is to simply press record in the Clip Slot of a Scene that Loops endlessly, and just keep recording into the single Clip until you have one or more takes you like; then go back and use the Clip Start/Stop values to trim your Clip to the take you want to keep. If you want to get rid of the other inferior takes, simply [ctrl-click/right-click] on the trimmed Clip and choose Crop Clip(s) from the contextual menu. This will save your trimmed Clip, discarding the rest.
- Devices such as the Akai APC40, APC20, and the Novation Launchpad allow for one-button Clip-recording initiation. Although it is not fully hands-free recording, I find it quite a bit easier to press a glowing button than to reach for a mouse or Track pad, aim, and click on a tiny button.
- Although it is possible to record to multiple Tracks simultaneously in Session View, it is challenging to start and stop recording a series of Clips in the Clip grid at the same time. I find it a lot easier to use Arrangement View for multitrack recording.

Recording in Arrangement View

Making an audio recording in Arrangement View is a much more "traditional" recording experience: you select where the recording will take place on the timeline, and execute the recording. The starting and stopping of recording can be controlled with the Loop/Punch Brace and/or a Count-In. There is no Global Quantize value to worry about, although the Snap to Grid value remains useful.

The process for making an audio (or MIDI) recording in Arrangement View can be summarized like this:

1. Arm a Track (or Tracks) for recording.
2. Select the desired input type, input channel, and monitoring mode in the In/Out section.
3. Check incoming audio levels and tone and adjust accordingly.
4. Enable the Global Record button in the Control Bar.
5. If desired, set Punch In and/or Punch Out points with the Loop Brace and enable the Punch In/Out switches. Otherwise, set the Arrangement Position at the location where you would like recording to begin.
6. Press Play to begin recording.
7. When you are done, press Stop.

Starting and/or Stopping Recording with Punch In/Out Points

The Loop Brace also serves another key purpose when recording audio or MIDI in Arrangement View: the Punch In/Out controls. These controls allow you to set a start and end point for your recordings, which can be helpful when you are recording yourself or when you want to overdub a short phrase of a specific length on a Track that already contains useful takes you want to keep. Particularly with Audio Clip recordings, which take up valuable hard-drive space, I have gotten into the habit of using the Punch In/Out Brace to record exactly the length I need and no more. Additionally, you can Loop-record multiple takes with the Loop Brace and then trim the recording to the best take.

Pic. 6b: The Loop/Punch controls in the Control Bar.

Using these controls could not be easier:

- Set the Loop Start/Punch In Point and Loop/Punch Length using one of the following methods:
- Click-and-drag to select a range of bars in the Arrangement that you plan to record to. Press [cmd-I/ctrl-I] to set the Loop Brace to Loop this selection, which is not what you want, but it puts the Loop Brace in the right place. In the Control Bar, deactivate the Loop switch and enable the Punch In/Out switches.
- Click-and-drag the Loop Brace Start/Stop triangles to the range of bars you want to record to. Enable the Punch In/Out switches in the Control Bar.
- Type or click-and-drag the desired recording start bar value into the Loop Start/Punch In Point box. Type in or click-and-drag the desired recording length into the Loop/Punch Length box. Enable the Punch In/Out switches in the Control Bar.
- Once you have the Punch values and switches set, place your insert point/ Arrangement Position a few bars before the Loop Brace.
- Enable Global Recording, and press Play.

When the Arrangement Position reaches the Punch In point, recording begins. When the Arrangement Position reaches the Punch Out point, recording stops but playback continues until you stop it manually.

Helpful Hints for Recording in Arrangement View

- Note that you do not need to activate both the Punch In and the Punch Out switches. In other words, you can specify where you want to begin recording without specifying an end point, so you can continue recording as long as you like. Or vice versa: Set a Punch Out point, but start recording right away, without a Punch In point.
- Even though you set a particular Punch In point, Live will still record from the point at which you started playback, and simply set the Clip Start at the Punch In point. This is good, in that any "inspired" moments leading up to the recording take are also captured and retrievable, but most of the time you will end up with several bars of silence at the beginning of your recordings taking up space on your hard drive. You can use the Crop Clip(s) function to solve this after recording.
- You can "Loop-record" by enabling the Loop switch in the Control Bar. Live will record your Looped takes sequentially into one file until you stop recording. Use the Undo/ Redo commands to step backward/forward through your takes to the one you want to use. Or, open the Loop-recorded Clip's Sample Editor to review all of the takes by moving the Loop Brace and Clip Start/End points. When you have the take selected that you want, you can use Crop Clip(s) to get rid of the other unused takes.
- Multitrack recording is as easy as arming multiple Tracks for recording before starting to record. You will, of course, have to make all the various logical settings in the In/ Out section for each Track. There is a setting in Preferences/Record Warp Launch for Exclusive Arming of Tracks that you may want to turn off, or you can simply override it by holding down [cmd/ctrl] as you click on the Arm buttons.
- Avoid moving faders and knobs on your controllers or adjusting Mixer or plug-in parameters while audio recording, because Live will record your gestures, assuming you want to save them as automation data. If this is intentional, then go for it, but I rarely find that I want to record audio and Track automation at the same time. Try to focus on getting a good recording of a good performance and worry about mixing details later.

Helpful Hints for Recording in Either View

- You can choose which file format your new recordings will be written to in Preferences > Record Warp Launch: File Type. The choices are WAV or AIFF. There is no appreciable difference between these file types: files recorded in either type will sound exactly the same and be exactly the same size.

- New recordings made in Live will be saved to your current Project's folder in Samples > Recorded. They are saved with the naming convention of "(recording number) (Track name).(extension)," so the fifth recording on a Track called Vocals would be saved as "0005 Vocals.wav."

- Be aware that the name of any new recording is taken from the name of the Track when the recording was made, and it will affect both the new Clip's name and the file name saved to your hard drive. It is a good idea to get in the habit of naming your Tracks before you start recording, otherwise you will end up with a lot of files named "0004 1 Audio.wav" or something similar, and when you go searching for that one amazing accordion recording you did last year, it will take you a long time to find it. Better still to rename the Track before each new recording so that the filenames are quite specific: "0011 Lead Vocals Verse 2 sm58.wav" is more descriptive than "0011 Vocals.wav." A little planning ahead will save you a lot of time down the road.

- You can save notes about a Track/recording: [ctrl-click/right-click] on the Track name and select Edit Info Text. I find that saving notes about which microphone/preamp/ special settings were used is useful later if you decide to redo or add to a recording.

- There is a Preference for setting the default Warp Mode assigned to new recordings: Preferences > Record Warp Launch: Default Warp Mode. If, for example, you know you will be recording a lot of vocals in a session, set the default Warp Mode to Tones, or perhaps Complex. This way, if the tempo of your Project changes later on, your recorded Clips will likely sound good without a lot of additional tinkering.

See the appendix sections for more information about audio, digital audio, and recording.

Chapter 7

MIXDOWN AND EXPORTING

Okay. You've finished your Arrangement, and it sounds great. Now you want to make a stereo file to play elsewhere. It is time for a mixdown. Go File > Export Audio/Video.

Pic. 7a: The Export Audio/Video dialog box.

Exporting Your Mix to a File

This dialog box will allow you to export audio (or video with audio) to a number of specifications. Let's walk through the various controls and then talk about useful settings for different applications.

The most important thing to remember about this dialog box is that it will export from exactly the state that Live was in when you invoked the Export Audio/Video command, so be sure to double-check that what is playing is what you want to export. Although we are currently talking about this function in the context of exporting a mixdown, you can use Export Audio/Video in a similar manner as the Resampling function. Here are some things to keep in mind about exporting:

- If you are in Arrangement View when you execute the export and you have neither a selection nor the Arrangement Loop switch enabled, Live will default to exporting the entire timeline from the start of the first Clip to the end of the last Clip. This is great for mixing down your entire Arrangement to a file.
- If you are in Arrangement View with a selection when you execute the export, Live will export the range of your selected bars. Use this to export a specific portion of the timeline.
- If you have the Arrangement Loop switch enabled when you execute the export, Live will export the Arrangement Loop's range of bars from the timeline.
- If you have Loops playing in Session View when you go to export, those will be played throughout your entire exported file in addition to Clips on the Arrangement timeline (if any). Clicking on Stop All Clips or the Back to Arrangement button before exporting will ensure that only what is playing in the Arrangement is exported.
- If you are in Session View when you export, Live will ask you how many bars you would like to export of the currently playing Clips. Use this to submix a group of Clips to a new Clip. Be aware that if you have Tracks playing in the Arrangement at the same time, these will be exported as well.
- If you have any Tracks soloed or deactivated at the time of exporting, these will be represented in the export in that state. Check to make sure that all the Tracks you want to export are playing the way you want them to before you export them.

Now let's have a look at the various controls in the Export Audio/Video dialog:

- Rendered Track—This pull-down controls which Track or Tracks you are sourcing for the export.
- Master—The Master Track's output will be used as the source for exporting.
- All Tracks—This handy setting will export each of your Tracks individually for the selected length. This is a great way to exchange files for mixing/remixing with someone who uses a DAW other than Live.
- Individual Tracks—This setting will export only the selected Track for the previously selected range of bars.
- Normalize—If selected, Live will Normalize the exported file. Normalization simply means to "turn the gain of the file up as high as it can go without clipping." Normalization does not employ dynamic compression or limiting—it is simply a volume adjustment. The highest peak in the file will be 0.00 dB after Normalization.
- Render as Loop—If you select this option, the exported file will contain all included effects as if the Loop had already been playing previously. In fact, Live plays through your selection once before beginning the export so that any time based effect tails, such as reverb or delay, will already be echoing out at the start of the Loop.

- File Type—Choose WAV or AIFF here.
- Convert to Mono—Select this if you would like to export a mono file.
- Sample Rate/Bit Depth—Choose the desired settings for your destination file (discussed below).
- Dither—Live offers five kinds of dither to choose from (discussed below).
- Create Analysis File—If you intend to use the exported file in a Live Set, enable this option and it will speed the importing of your file.

Using Dither

- Dither is a very low-level amount of noise that can be applied when you are exporting to a lower bit depth than you are presently using, and can help smooth the loss of resolution. The trick is to do it only once in the entire life of your song: multiple layers of dither will degrade your sound quality. Here are some guidelines:
- If you are exporting a file that you intend to use again in a Set, export at the same bit depth you are currently using and do not apply dither.
- If you are exporting a mix to send out for mastering by a pro, export at the same bit depth you are currently using and do not apply dither.
- If you are exporting at a higher bit depth than you are currently using, do not add dither.
- In short, the only time you should apply dither is when you are exporting your absolute final mixdown that will not be changed again in any way, and you are lowering the bit depth during the export (for example, from 32 bits that you have been working at in Live down to 16 bits for burning to an audio CD).
- If you have been working at 32 bit and your final mix output will be 24 bit, you should add dither here as well—but again, only if this is the very last operation that will be performed on the file.
- Here are your dither options:
- Triangular/Rectangular—Provided by Ableton, these two are the safest to use if you think there may be any possibility of making additional changes to the exported file.
- POW-r 1, 2 and 3—These three industry-standard dither types offer increasing amounts of dither that sits above the frequency range of human hearing. Use one of these when you are certain that your file will not be altered after exporting.

Exporting Guidelines

- The Export Audio/Video dialog box offers a lot of options. Here are some optimal settings for various tasks:
- If you are exporting a file that you intend to use again in your current Set (or another Set), export at the sample rate and bit depth you are currently using, which will be the default settings in the Export dialog box. Do not apply dither.
- If you are exporting a mixdown that you intend to play out of Live as part of a DJ set, again, export at the sample rate and bit depth you are currently using, which will be the default settings in the Export dialog box. Do not apply dither. There is no need to reduce sample rate and bit depth if you are not going to burn an audio CD.
- If you are exporting a mixdown that will be sent to a mastering studio for processing, call them and ask what audio file specifications they prefer and ask if they can work with 32-bit files. More than likely, they will tell you to export at the sample rate and bit depth you are currently working at, and to not apply dither.

- If you are exporting a mixdown that you intend to make an MP3 of, export at the sample rate and bit depth you are currently using, which will be the default settings in the Export dialog box. Do not apply dither. The MP3 encoder—such as iTunes, for example—will do a better job of making the MP3 with the higher resolution source than if you had first exported to a 16-bit, 44,100 Hz sample-rate file.
- If you are exporting a mix for burning to an audio CD, this is the only time to reduce the sample rate to 44,100 Hz, the bit depth to 16 bit, and add POW-r dither.

Chapter **8**

BEST PRACTICES

If you intend to spend a lot of time with Live, you will want to immerse yourself deeper and deeper into the tool. Mastery of anything consists of living and breathing your craft. And with Live that means using it to make music for sure, but also for keeping up with updates, file management, knowing what all the Preferences do, visiting the Ableton website and forums, and keeping up with the greater community.

What follows here is wisdom distilled from having used the program regularly for a few years.

Ableton Live Preferences

The Preferences seem complex when you first start using them, but before long, you should grow to know them all intimately. I have met users who complain about a particular feature, and when I say, "Well, you know there's a Preference for that, right?" their eyes bulge and they shower me with thanks, as if I unlocked some magic treasure chest for them. But it is all right there—you just have to be willing to look.

I will elaborate here on only the Preferences that are exceptionally useful, are not self-explanatory, or could benefit from more detail:

Look/Feel

- Skin—Probably the most popular Preference award would have to go to the Skin chooser, which is on this page. It may seem hokey at first, but when you spend long hours in front of the same interface, making it easy on the eyes is no small matter. As well, there have been times when I get stuck on a song and will flip to a random skin and keep working. Try it. Sometimes a fresh visual perspective can seriously reframe your creativity.
- Zoom Display—This is a newer Preference that can solve a lot of eyestrain issues and allows you to customize the view for your monitor and viewing distance. Now, if I could just assign this value to my mouse wheel!

- Hide Labels—A nontrivial switch. Once you get a big session going, reclaiming even a little screen real estate is a cause for joy, and once you know what everything does, Hide Labels will clean things up a bit in Session View.
- Follow Behavior—This is a matter of taste, or "preference," if you like! I find I use the Page setting the most, as it seems less taxing on my system and eyesight.

Audio

Undoubtedly the most used Preference page on my system. Get to know it well.

The Audio tab in Live's Preferences offers you control over how Live interacts with your audio interface. You may find that you need to continue experimenting with the settings on this page until you get your setup to an optimized state. This is normal, so do what you can to get comfortable with the variables on this page. See the appendices on digital audio and on latency for even more detail.

- Audio Driver Type—The first step is to choose the audio driver type from the first pull-down menu. If your audio interface has multiple driver types, consult its manual about which driver type you should use. If you are unsure, try one and see if your Device shows up in the Input/Output pull-downs in the next step.
- Audio Input Device and Audio Output Device—Select your sound card in these pull-down lists.

Your audio interface comes with some number of audio inputs and outputs, typically some combination of each between 2 and 18. Some inputs and outputs may be analog, some digital. The next two steps will allow you to choose which ones you want to work with in Live:

- Click on the Input Config button. If you chose your Device in the Input/Output Device selectors, the selected Device's available audio inputs should be listed here. Depending on your Device and driver, your inputs may be listed here twice: as individual mono channels and as stereo pairs. The choices you make here will dictate which mono and/or stereo inputs you have available for recording on your Audio Tracks in Live's In/Out section of the Mixer. You can select any/all of the inputs you plan to use with Live, but keep in mind that every input you enable here does utilize some of your system's resources, so it is a good idea to enable only the inputs you actually plan to use. You can always come back and enable more inputs as you need them later. Press OK when you are done.
- Click on the Output Config button. The same rules apply here as they do for inputs. You may decide that you need only one pair of outputs for sending Live's output to your speakers. Then again, you may be doing some external processing or working in a multispeaker surround environment. Again, enable only the outputs you actually plan to use. Click on OK when done.

Sample Rate

Your audio interface will likely be able to operate at a number of sample rates. Sample rate represents the number of amplitude measurements taken in a given second of recording by your audio interface. Reduced to its simplest terms, the higher the sample-rate setting, the higher the quality of the recordings you make, and the higher the quality of all internal processing done to the files, such as plug-ins, volume, panning, and so on. At the same time, the higher the sample rate, the larger the recorded file size will be, and the more computational power your computer will need to work with your files. If you work with a sample library whose sample rate is largely 44,100 Hz, or if your computer is an older model, try starting with a sample rate of 44,100 Hz. If your computer can handle working with higher sample rates, by all means, do. But if you find that your computer is struggling for resources when you are working on a reasonably complex Set, try lowering the sample rate to 44,100 Hz for future Sets. See a more detailed description of "sample rate" in the appendix on digital audio.

Bit Depth

One of the more important settings for audio is not found on the Audio tab. It is on the Record/Warp/Launch tab, and it is called Bit Depth. This setting works together with the Sample Rate setting to determine the file size and resolution (quality) of your recordings and processing. Bit Depth determines the resolution of each amplitude measurement taken by your audio interface when recording. The choices here are 16, 24, or 32. To a greater degree yet than sample rate, I encourage you to work at the highest setting your computer can handle. The file sizes will be bigger than 16-bit recordings, but they will benefit from wider dynamic range, more detail, and a lower noise floor. My advice is to start at 32 bits and take it downward if you find that your computer is struggling with it. See a more detailed description of Bit Depth in the appendix on digital audio.

Buffer Size

Your computer has a temporary repository of data that it holds in memory before handing it to, or taking it from, your audio interface. The size of this temporary repository is called the "buffer size." The lower the setting, the less delay (known as "latency") there will be as audio travels in and out of your computer, but the more of your computer's resources it will require. As the buffer size goes up, it becomes less taxing on your computer, but the latency for audio passing through increases. The best way to go about setting this is to start with it low and increase it as necessary. If you encounter clicks and pops while you are working, come back and raise the buffer size until the clicks go away.

Handily, Live provides you with a way to test this setting without ever leaving the Preferences window:

1. Set your buffer size as high as it will go.
2. At the bottom of the Audio Preferences tab is a Test section. Take the CPU Usage Simulator to 90%.
3. Turn on the Test Tone generator. You can adjust the tone's volume and frequency to your liking, but for this test, only a comfortable volume is required and the defaults may be just fine.
4. Lower the buffer size until the Test Tone starts to audibly distort. You must press Apply after each adjustment. When the tone starts to distort, raise the buffer size in small increments until it no longer distorts. This is the lowest buffer size that your computer will be able to handle at near maximum CPU load. Remember this setting.

These settings are conservative, so they will work at any CPU load without your needing to change them. However, if you are making a recording and the CPU load is lower than 90%, and you need to reduce latency for recording, you can and should.

If you are just mixing and not recording, you can safely turn your buffer size up as high as it will go to put the least amount of strain on your computer and put all your resources toward making complex mixes with lots of plug-ins and software instruments. You will lose some responsiveness from Live's transport controls as you increase the buffer size—stopping and starting will be a bit more sluggish because it takes longer to fill the larger buffer—but your system will be as stable as possible. Note that this buffer size setting will be different for different audio interfaces and at different sample-rate and bit-depth settings. You may want to start a list of workable settings for each interface you plan to use.

See a more detailed discussion of managing latency in your recording process in the appendix section.

MIDI Sync

This is the second most used Preference page, if you work with MIDI Devices. These settings will be covered in detail in the companion book, Sound Design, Mixing, and Mastering with Ableton Live, which deals with MIDI in great detail.

File Folder

Lots of goodies on this page:

- Save Current Set as Default—This one is quite useful and is covered later in this chapter in the "Templates" section.
- Create Analysis Files—This switch is a trade-off between speed and clutter: if it is turned on, Live will create an analysis file (.asd) for any audio file loaded into a Set. This tiny file sits in the same folder as the audio file and has the same name as the audio file, but with the .asd extension. It contains information about the file's tempo and waveform, and this will greatly speed the future loading of the paired audio file into a Set. For longer files, this time savings is noticeable, and when you click on the Save button in the Clip View panel, Live will save all your Clip settings to the .asd file. The trade-off, however, is the creation of literally thousands of additional files on your hard drive. I just did a search for .asd files on my laptop and found 10,000+ of them, totaling 500+ MB. I guess it comes down to the question of how much hard-drive space your time is worth to you.
- Sample Editor—If you own a sample-editing program such as BIAS Peak or Steinberg WaveLab, you can specify its location here. Then, when you click on the Edit button in a Clip's Sample panel, it will launch this editor and open that Clip's audio for editing. You can make destructive changes in this external editor, resave the file, and return to Live where the changes will be reflected.
- Temporary Folder—The location you set here will determine where new, unsaved Set data will live until you save it. If you open a new Set and make a recording, it will be saved here. You will want to clean out this folder from time to time, and you must do it manually.
- Maximum Cache Size and Cleanup—If you attempt to import a file type other than a WAV or an AIFF, such as an MP3 for example, Live will have to turn it into a WAV or an AIFF format before it can use the file. The decoded files live at this location, as do temporary files used during installations of updates and such. You can limit the total size of these cache files, as well as delete them periodically with the Cleanup button.
- Rescan Plug-ins—If you add, move, or remove plug-ins from your plug-ins folders outside of Live while Live is running, you can click on this button to have Live rescan the folders and relist them.
- Use Audio Units/Use VST Plug-Ins System Folders (Mac only)—AU plug-in files (.component) and VST plug-in files (.vst) are stored in Library/Audio/Plug-Ins/AU or VST, respectively, and are shared by all applications that use these plug-in types. Live's use of the plug-ins in these two system folders can be turned on/off with these switches, which can be helpful when trying to isolate a buggy plug-in that is crashing Live.

- VST Custom Folder (Mac only)—In addition to this system library VST folder, you can specify a second VST folder for plug-ins here. Some uses of this second folder could include the following:
- To have a separate folder of VST plug-ins that you use only with Live.
- To have a second folder of newly installed freeware/betaware VSTs that you are still testing for stability. This way, you can always turn off the Preference for using this additional folder when doing mission-critical work or when performing live, for which having stability is essential. When a new plug-in has proven stable, move it to the main VST folder in the system Library. I like to keep an alias (shortcut) to both VST folders on my desktop (or in the Finder sidebar) so that when I get new VST plug-ins, they can easily be placed in one of these two folders.

Record Warp Launch

Some of these Preferences have been mentioned in chapter 6, "Recording Audio with Live," but let's cover a few more of them here.

- Exclusive Arm/Solo—Enabling either Arm or Solo causes Live to arm or solo just one Track at a time. If you select Arm or Solo on a second Track, Live will switch the arm or solo to the new Track rather than arm or solo them both. You can still override this Preference by holding down the [cmd/ctrl] key while clicking on either button to arm or solo multiple Tracks. Handily, the opposite is also true: if this Preference is disabled, Live will arm or solo as many Tracks as you click on, and you can still override this with a [cmd-click/ctrl-click] to force a single arm or solo at a time.
- Loop/Warp Short Samples—This setting determines how Live will handle the importing of new, short Audio Clips. The Auto setting works for my needs most of the time, but if you work with one kind of file a lot—one-shot drums on the timeline, for example—you can make another choice here that will be more useful for you.
- Auto Warp Long Samples—Long samples can take a while to auto-Warp, so if you don't often want long samples to be Warped to tempo, turn this second setting off—importing will be far faster.
- Default Warp Mode—Beats makes sense if you use a lot of drum Loops, but perhaps you make a lot of ambient music and prefer the sound of tones. Perhaps you have enough CPU to always use Complex or Complex Pro by default. A well-chosen setting here can save a lot of extra clicking in Clip View.
- Create Fades on Clip Edges—Enabling this puts a 4 ms fade-in/-out on all Audio Clips to avoid clicks and pops that happen with poorly trimmed samples. It works, I can't hear it happening, and so I've always left it enabled.
- Start Recording on Launch—This setting is discussed briefly in chapter 6, "Recording Audio with Live." Enabling it will allow you to start Clips—even multiple Clips—recording by launching a Scene. If you have a group jamming to a Loop or the metronome, launching a Scene with one or more armed Tracks will begin recording Clips to the empty Clip Slots. This could also be useful for recording multiple takes of a section to multiple Clip Slots triggered with a footpedal.

CPU

- Multicore/Multiprocessor Support—Definitely leave this setting enabled if you have multiple processors/cores. This allows Live to spread the computational load out among these CPUs.
- Plug-In Buffer Size—Unless you come up with a scenario in which you are directed by Ableton to change this setting, leave it set to As Audio Buffer.

Library

- Change Library Location—With this function you can either move the location of your Live Library or create a new Library from scratch if you are having problems with your current one and Repair Library does not fix the problem.

Resource Management

There are a number of places in Live where you can manage Live's usage of your computer's resources. Understanding how Live uses these resources will allow you to make prudent trade-offs between quality and stability.

CPU Load Meter

Pic. 8a: The CPU Load Meter in the Control Bar.

The percentile bar gives you feedback about how hard your computer is working to reproduce the current Set's audio and MIDI calculations. Keep in mind that every aspect of the program—from playing back a file to changing volume to an EQ plug-in—is math, and as your Set gets more complex, so does the math to play it back properly. There are many components of your computer working in concert to carry out the tasks that you are requesting of it, and your computer is only as fast as its weakest link. Read appendix D, "The Makings of a DAW," for more detail on this subject. Here is a list of the things that contribute to an overloaded CPU load meter:

- Non-Live background functions—Turn off any other nonnecessary background applications while Live is running. Every running application consumes CPU that could be devoted to Live instead. I've known some people who even disable their network capabilities to keep the CPU load meter down even further.
- Sample Rate and Bit Depth settings—The choices you select in your Preferences about which sample rate and bit depth you are choosing to work with will greatly affect the CPU load meter. Any calculation on an 88,200 Hz sample-rate file will take twice as much math to accomplish as a 44,100 Hz file. The same goes for bit depth, so a 88,200 Hz sample rate 32-bit file takes roughly four times the math of its 44,100 Hz, 16-bit counterpart. So these two settings are a trade-off between audio quality and Track quantity.
- Plug-ins and Instruments—Every plug-in Device is a series of math algorithms. The more complex the plug-in, the more math-intensive it is and the harder it is on your CPU to run it. Live's own plug-ins are optimized to be as low overhead as possible, but they add up. Third-party plug-ins and Instruments can range from being very light to being CPU vampires. The easiest way to tell what impact a plug-in Device is having on your CPU is to bypass it while Live is playing and see how much CPU load is recovered. If you find a Device that is hogging resources, you can disable it, replace it with another lighter plug-in, or "Freeze" the Track to recover some CPU power (see the next section for more on Freezing and Flattening). Aside from getting a faster CPU, having as much RAM as possible installed on your computer will allow you to run more plug-ins and Instruments simultaneously.

- Hi-Quality mode for some Audio Effects—Four of Live's plug-ins have a Hi-Quality mode that will add some audio quality at the expense of CPU. These are the EQ Eight, Flanger, Dynamic Tube, and Saturator. By default, these Devices have Hi-Quality mode disabled when you add them, but you can save their default settings with Hi-Quality mode turned on if you choose to. To toggle this mode on or off, [ctrl-click/right-click] on the title bar of the Device and select Hi-Quality mode from the contextual menu. You will see the Save As Default option there as well. Additionally, note that the Reverb plug-in has three modes of its own, each with increasing quality and computational complexity: Eco, Mid, and High.
- High-Quality Rate Conversion—In any Audio Clip View there is a Hi-Q button in the Sample panel that is enabled by default. This button governs the algorithms used for pitch transposition and real-time sample-rate conversion to the current sample rate. Disabling this button on Clips that are transposed or are being sample-rate converted will regain some CPU at the expense of some audio quality.

Pic. 8b: The Hi-Q High-Quality Rate Conversion button in Audio Clip View.

- Complex/Complex Pro Warp modes—Warping is definitely a CPU-intensive task, and these two Warp Modes multiply that complexity considerably. The default Warp Mode is Beats in Live's Preferences, which is one of the lightest on the CPU. Change this to one of the Complex modes only if you have the CPU overhead to do so. Another option is to Freeze Warped Tracks to recover a bit of CPU (see the next section, "Freeze Track," for more on Freezing and Flattening).
- Audio Interface I/O—Every enabled input and output on your audio interface will contribute to the CPU load meter. If you aren't using an input or output, disable it on the Audio Preferences tab to recover some CPU. See chapter 6, "Recording Audio with Live," for more on setting up your audio interface.

Audio playback functions are given the highest priority of all functions in Live. So when Live is reaching its CPU limits, other "secondary" functions (such as screen redraws of the interface) may become sluggish before you hear any audio dropouts. This is a good thing, as an audience won't mind if your screen redraws are sluggish!

Freeze Track

There will be times when you run low on CPU, even when heeding all of the above advice. Your only option at that point is to remove some Devices or to use Freeze Track to recover some CPU. Freezing is a function that turns your computation-heavy Tracks, such as Instruments and complex Racks, into comparatively straightforward Audio Tracks by "printing" the Device's output to one or more audio files and then disabling the original Devices. While the result is quite similar to recording or "resampling" a Track's output to another Track, Freezing has the significant benefit of being reversible. Freezing can be done on any Track, and the amount of CPU recovery will depend on the complexity and number of Devices that you are Freezing.

To Freeze a Track that is CPU intensive, select the Track in question and do one of the following:

- [Ctrl-click/right-click] on the Track and choose Freeze Track from the contextual menu.
- Go Edit > Freeze.

When you do this, Live will present a progress bar as the chosen Track is rendered to an audio file. This file is saved in the Project Folder > Samples > Processed > Freeze folder. If you Unfreeze a Track and make even one change to a Device on the Track and re-Freeze it, a new audio file is created. When you are done working on a Project, it is a good idea to manually delete unused Frozen files, or use the File Manager (described later in this chapter) to remove the unused files.

Pic. 8c: Various parts of a Frozen Track.

When the Freeze Track operation is complete, the Frozen Track will now appear an icy blue color in Session View and Arrangement View, and so will all Devices on the Track in Track View. Now that the Track is Frozen, all Device automation has been printed to audio, and no additional changes can be made to any of the Track's Devices without first Unfreezing the Track. However, here is a list of operations that still can be performed to a Frozen Track:

- Edit, cut, copy, paste, duplicate, and trim Clips.
- Draw and edit mixer automation and mixer Clip Envelopes.
- Consolidate.
- Record Session View Clip launches into the Arrangement View.
- Create, move, and duplicate Session View Scenes.
- Drag Frozen MIDI Clips into Audio Tracks.

Important! Note that edits such as cutting and pasting sections of a Frozen Track will not cause the Frozen Track's temporal effects to be recalculated and re-Frozen, so you may end up with some unexpected reverb or delay tails. To avoid this, Unfreeze the Track first, make the edits, and re-Freeze the Track.

Frozen Tracks can be Unfrozen to make changes, which can be accomplished by selecting the desired Track(s) and doing one of the following:

- [Ctrl-click/right-click] on the Track and choose Unfreeze Track from the contextual menu.
- Go Edit > Unfreeze.

Unfrozen Tracks regain all their original editing properties, as well as re-incurring their original CPU load.

As a Set becomes more CPU intensive than your computer can handle, try Freezing a Track that is complex in its number and type of Devices and is a Track that you may not need to make a lot of changes to. If you run into further CPU limitations, continue to Freeze more Tracks. You may get into a more sluggish work flow of Freezing and Unfreezing Tracks as needed, but this workaround will allow you to work on complex Sets far beyond what your computer would otherwise be capable of.

Flattening Tracks

Flattening a Track consists of taking a previously Frozen Track and permanently transforming it to an Audio Track. All notes, Instruments, effects, and Device automation is printed to one or more Audio Clips, and all Devices previously on the Track are deleted. CPU recovery is permanent, but undoing can only be accomplished by stepping backward through the Undo history to a point before Flattening.

To Flatten a Frozen Track, select the Frozen Track and do one of the following:

- [Ctrl-click/right-click] on the Track and choose Flatten from the contextual menu.
- Go Edit > Flatten.

While the Flatten command's undoable nature may seem disadvantageous, keep in mind that you can import Tracks from previous Sets, so if you save a version of the Set just before Flattening, you can always reimport the un-Flattened Track at that state in the future. (There is more about importing Tracks and Clips from other Sets later in this chapter.) Flattened Tracks also reacquire all the usual editing capabilities of a typical Audio Track, such as reversing, transposition, Warping, ans so on, so these are more reasons that you might opt to Flatten a Track.

Hard-disk Overload Indicator and RAM Mode

Just as it is possible to overrun your CPU's ability to keep up with computational tasks, it is equally possible to overload your hard drive with data read/write operations. This is unrelated to running out of space on your hard drive, which is also a possible issue, of course. Instead, the Disk Overload Indicator comes on when your hard drive has exceeded its ability to keep up with storage and retrieval requests.

Pic. 8d: The Disk Overload Indicator in the Control Bar.

A hard drive can read and/or write only so much data at a time. Standard-issue hard drives (especially laptops) spin at a slower speed of 5,400 rpm, as opposed to the faster, media-optimized drives that spin at 7,200 rpm. In essence, the faster the rotational speed, the more read/write operations the drive can accommodate simultaneously, and the more heat they tend to put off. (See more detail about this in appendix D, "The Makings of a DAW.") So the primary solution to disk-overload challenges is to be working with a fast hard drive to begin with.

Some other solutions to disk overload include the following:

- Turn off any other background applications that might try to access the hard drive while Live is running, including virus scanning, auto-saving, network sharing, file downloads/uploads, and so on. For maximum potential, quit all unnecessary applications other than Live.
- Reduce the number of audio channels by recording in mono instead of stereo.
- Reduce the number of audio channels by merging Audio Clips using "resampling."
- Place some of your shorter Audio Clips into Clip RAM mode, which will store the Audio Clip in RAM rather than reading it repeatedly from the hard drive. Use this option carefully, because every Clip you put into RAM mode will then contribute to your overall CPU load.

Pic. 8e: The Clip RAM mode button in Clip View.

Device Delay Compensation

Every plug-in or Instrument Device incurs a measureable amount of latency in addition to adding to the overall CPU usage. Literally, the math involved in a plug-in doing its job takes time, and so an audio signal that passes through the plug-in arrives later than if the plug-in were bypassed. Thankfully, all of the calculations to keep your signals in step with each other are handled by Live internally through a process called Device Delay Compensation. While this is a selectable option in the Options menu, it should be left on in most instances. Without it, Tracks with a lot of plug-ins will fall noticeably out of sync with the rest of your Set.

File Management

Using a computer to produce music, you will quickly discover how crucial file management becomes: buying, storing, and organizing a sample library; naming, organizing, sharing, and backing up Sets; recording multiple takes of each section of each Track to new files; rendering mix, submix, and resampled files; Live's Library, Presets, templates, and Live Packs . . . there are a lot of files to keep track of! Herein is a collection of best practices for keeping your files functional. But first, a word about quality source materials.

Digital Audio File Types and Data Compression

If you were building a house that you intended to live in, you would likely not go to the lumber yard and buy the cheapest materials you could find. You would instinctively know that a quality house requires quality materials. The same concept applies to making music: you want to make and work with the best recordings possible. There is a time-honored phrase in the audio-engineering community that sums this idea up nicely: "Crap in, crap out." Meaning, if you start with compromised quality, you will end up with compromised quality.

Due to the advent of the Internet, data-compressed audio files such as the MP3 have become a ubiquitous delivery format. The standard 128 kilobits per second (kbps) MP3 is 11 times smaller in size than an uncompressed 16-bit, 44.1 kHz CD quality WAV file you would find on a CD. Think about that: take away 90 percent of the data, but still try to maintain the original's quality! The data compression used to make an MP3 definitely compromises the sound quality, but it is also amazing that it works at all!

The key phrase in the above paragraph is that an MP3 is a "delivery format," not a source format. When you are completely done with a mix (including final mixing and mastering at the highest resolution possible), then, and only then, is it time to make a low-resolution MP3 out of something if you must for delivery online. Even though Live supports them as an input type, you want to avoid using Loops, samples, or recordings that are in a compressed file type (MP3, AAC, OGG, or FLAC) in your Live Sets if at all possible. Playback and mixing of one or two MP3s for DJ'ing is marginally passable in a pinch. Mixing together many sections of many MP3s and trying to make a quality mix or remix is to fight a serious uphill battle. You will never achieve the results you are seeking if you start with compressed file types. Do a comparison between a WAV file and an MP3 sometime and be prepared to be amazed.

When you import a compressed file type into Live, the first thing Live does is to convert it to a WAV or an AIF for use in your Set, but do not be fooled into thinking that this somehow restores lost audio quality. This is the equivalent to taking a recorded cassette and making a CD from it: it will simply be a quality recording of a low-quality source. There is no program or Device in the world that can restore an MP3 to its original quality. Lossy compression is a one-way ticket.

Making quality music means using uncompressed Pulse Code Modulated files, which typically come in two flavors on personal computers: WAVE (.wav) and AIFF (.aif). These are the two formats that Live records in, and they are virtually identical in every way. They will each produce identical levels of quality at your chosen sample rate and bit depth. Look for, and make source materials in, these two formats. They may cost more and take up more hard-drive space, but isn't your music worth it?

You will also encounter a few application-specific file types such as REX files and file types designed for specific samplers; these are also uncompressed and perfectly acceptable to use for their given purpose.

Live Project Folders

The pivotal crossroad for files used in Live is the Project folder. It is the point of file creation, integration and processing, and may also be the destination for file exports such as resampling and rendered mixdown exports. Like your bedroom, a Project folder can be either a relaxing expression of Zen minimalism or a virtual disaster area requiring protective wear and a backhoe to navigate. How you choose to keep your files (and your bedroom!) is up to you, but here are some tools for making sense of everything.

A Project folder consists of the following:

- The Ableton Project Info folder—a folder used by Live to store several small files needed to run the Project. Do not use or delete this folder.
- Live Sets—The Live Sets that are contained by the Project, often iterations of a single song, set, show or idea, but not necessarily so.
- Presets folder—If you save any Live Device Preset to a Current Project folder (there is one of these inside every Live Device Preset list), Live will make a new Presets folder in your Project folder that will contain your saved Presets.
- The Samples folder—Audio files created by the Project's Sets.
- Imported—Files imported to the Live Set from elsewhere, but were copied to the Project folder at some point as the result of a Collect All and Save command.
- Processed—Files created by Live as a result of some processing action. Live creates subfolders for each of these processes, such as:
  - Consolidate—Any audio files that are consolidated together will show up here as a single new file.
  - Freeze—Frozen Tracks will render their results here. Each new Freeze is a new file.
  - Reverse—Clips that have been reversed with the Reverse button in Clip View will write a new file here.
- Waveforms—Any samples used in a Simpler, Sampler, or Impulse that were copied here as the result of a Collect All and Save command.

But a Set can reference audio and MIDI files from anywhere outside the Project folder as well. For example, you might choose to use additional audio from the following places:

- The Live Library
- Your own sample library from purchased data CDs, from DVDs, downloaded from websites, or recorded in the field
- Your own digital music library, perhaps consisting of MP3s
- Other Sets you have made
- Audio files on a server on your local network

In essence, you might use an audio file from anywhere you can get your hands on it! When you drag a file into a Live Set, one of two things happens:

- If the file is already in an uncompressed file format that Live can use natively (AIFF, WAV, REX, SDII [Mac]), Live will simply use the file as is, and the source file stays where it is.
- If the file is a compressed file type that Live recognizes (MP3, AAC, Ogg Vorbis, Ogg FLAC, or FLAC), the file is quickly decoded into a new WAV or AIFF that is stored in Live's Decoding Cache. The original file stays where it is.

Note that in neither case is the imported file moved or copied into the Project folder, added to the Live Library, or also put in your own sample library. This is both good and not so good:

- It is good because you likely want the original file to stay where it is: perhaps it is part of another Project, the Live Library, your own sample library, or your music library, and moving it would harm other uses of the file.
- It is not so good because the files needed for your current Project are not all kept together in one place, and if any of those external files are moved, renamed or deleted, your current Project will no longer work properly. Also, if you share the Project folder with someone, it will not have all the files needed to play properly on their system.

The only files that are stored by default in a Project folder's Samples folder are the ones created or modified within the process of building you Set. These include the following:

- Audio that's been recorded into your Set from an external input or that's been Resampled between Tracks.
- Frozen, Flattened, consolidated, and reversed Clips

The remaining audio files used in your Set stay where they are—unless you tell Live to do otherwise, such as using the following function, Collect All and Save.

Collect All and Save

Collect All and Save is an invaluable function in the File menu that copies external files currently in use in the Set into the Project's Samples folder. This function makes the Project folder self-contained so that it may be moved and used elsewhere or backed up to an archive without potentially having to Track down missing external files later. You should use this function when doing the following:

- You are going to share your Project with someone else.
- You are going to use the same Set on another computer that may not have all the same files.
- You are going to archive the Project and want to make sure that the archive is self-contained.

When the function is invoked, a dialog comes up that asks you which file types you want to collect into the Project folder.

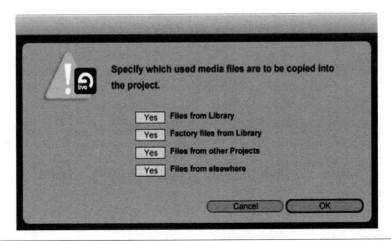

Pic. 8f: The Collect All and Save dialog box

You may choose any or all of the four source locations:

- Files from Library
- Factory Files from Library
- Files from other Projects
- Files from elsewhere

If, for example, you know you are going to reopen the Set on another computer and you know that the second computer has identical Factory Library Files, you could deselect that box and opt not to collect copies of those files to the Project folder, as they would be redundant if they were in both locations.

In my experience, I tend to share Projects with other musicians a lot, and I try to be vigilant about making regular backups of important Projects. I also find that the Audio Clips that are most regularly external to my Projects tend to be small audio files, such as Loops, one-shot drum hits, REX files, and short recordings from my own sample library. So on both counts, Collect All and Save has become part of my standard work flow and it has saved me on many occasions.

The only time I find that I intentionally avoid Collect All and Save is when I have a series of Projects that all reference the same large files, such as DJ Set, or a performance Set of rendered high-resolution stems. In these instances, Collect All and Save would only serve to make redundant copies of large files that are already being backed up anyway, and this would waste time and hard-drive space.

File Manager and Missing Files

The more advanced version of Collect All and Save and many other useful functions, can be found in the File Manager, which can be invoked in one of several ways:

- Go File > Manage Files.
- Go View > File Manager.
- [Ctrl-click/right-click] on any Project folder, Set, Preset, sample, or Live Library file and choose Manage File from the contextual menu.

The File Manager gives you access to a whole platter of delicious file-management tasks, including the following:

- Discovering and deleting unused consolidated, recorded, or Frozen files that may have accumulated in your Samples folder and are just wasting space.
- A more detailed Collect All and Save type operation.
- A list of Clips and Presets used in your Project.
- Listing missing files and a way to refind and relink them.
- Exporting Clips and Projects to the Library for future use.
- Creating compact Live Packs for sharing Live Projects with others.
- Working with and repairing your Library.

All of these functions eventually come in handy, but your first use may be when you open a Live Set and discover that you have missing files. Missing files occur when you move, rename, or delete files in use by your Live Project. Often this happens due to actions done outside of Live, such as when you are reorganizing your sample library's file structure for some well-intentioned reason. Then you reopen a Live Set and Live cannot find the files needed by the current Project. If you still have the files but they have just moved, do not panic—you can easily relink them with the File Manager's missing files search tool. If you no longer have the missing file, well . . .

Importing Sets, Tracks, and Clips

This extremely useful set of functions is also intuitively easy to use. Let's say you are working on a Set and you find that you want to import a Clip, a Track, or even another entire Set into this Set. Piece of cake:

- In one of the Live File Browsers, navigate to find the Set that contains the elements you want to import.
- If you want to import the entire Set, drag the Set icon onto the empty area after your last Track. The entire Set is imported to new Tracks, including all Tracks, Clips, Devices, and automation.
- If you want to import a Track, click on the expansion triangle next to the Set icon to see a list of that Set's available Tracks. Drag one of the Track icons onto the empty area after your last Track. That Track's Clips, Devices, and automation are imported onto a new Track.
- If you want to import a single Clip, open the expansion triangle next to the Track that contains the Clip you want to import in order to see a list of its available Clips. Drag the desired Clip onto a Track or onto the empty area after your last Track to put it on a new Track.

The Live Library

Think of the Live Library in much the same way you would a traditional library with books: The sounds and files in the Library are there to be accessed by all your Sets. Just as a librarian curates the books in a library with care and detail, handle your Live Library with the same consideration. Do not arbitrarily move, rename, or delete items in the Library unless you are sure of what you are doing. If your Library is having problems, try using the Repair Library function in Preferences > Library.

Having said that, there are some great uses for the Library. They include the following:

- The ability to save a new default Set—This very handy function is initiated from the first button on the Preferences/File Folder page, and it will save your current Set as the default New Set. Once you establish a favorite way of working, you can make a template blank Set that has all of your favorite settings predefined:
    - Your favorite input/output setup customized for your audio interface
    - Preset Devices, like EQs and Compressors on every Track, a favorite Impulse or Drum Rack ready to go on a MIDI Track, or a favorite mastering Audio Effect Rack on your Master Track.
    - Preset favorite Track Groups, names, and colors
    - Predefined computer key mappings and MIDI mappings specific to your Devices and way of working
- Saving default sample drop actions—You can customize what Live will do when you drop an audio file on an Audio Track's Track View or on a Drum Rack's empty cell. Either of these actions typically create a Simpler Device, and if you have favorite settings that you find yourself using regularly within this Device, you can save them as a default by doing the following:
    - Create an empty Simpler (or Sampler if you own it)
    - Adjust the parameters as you like
    - Drag the edited Device to either the On Drum Rack or On Track View folder, which can be found in the Browser at Library > Defaults > Dropping Samples

- Saving new Slice To New MIDI Track Presets—Live ships with several Slice To New MIDI Track Presets that do some pretty amazing things. If you want to create your own Presets for this function, do the following:
  - Create an empty Drum Rack.
  - Add an empty Simpler or Sampler to the Drum Rack to create a single Chain.
  - Add any additional MIDI or Audio Effects to this Chain.
  - Adjust parameters in any of the Devices.
  - Assign Macro Controls to any of the controls in the Chain's Devices.
- Drag the entire Drum Rack to the Library > Defaults > Slicing folder.
- Saving Presets for Live Devices to the Library—When you save a Preset from any Live Device, it is saved to your Library unless you specifically choose to save it to the Current Project folder in a Live Device Preset list. Presets saved to the Library will be available to any future Sets, while Presets saved to the Current Project are only immediately available to that Project.
- Ableton Live Packs and Factory Live Packs (.alp files)—An Ableton Live Pack is a means for packing and compressing Projects and additional Library content for archiving or distribution as a single file. Live Projects can be made into Live Packs via the File Manager's Manage Project page. A Live Pack has the .alp extension, and has the benefit of being up to 50 percent smaller than the Project folder that was used to create it. An .alp file can be unpacked simply by double-clicking on it or dropping it onto an open Live Set. While unpacking, Live will ask you where you want to store the unpacked content. If the Live Pack contains files that I might use in future Projects, I will unpack it into a folder I made in the Library called "Live Packs." Ableton will often distribute new Library content (new Instrument Devices, samples, Presets, and so on) in the form of a Live Pack, and these are called Factory Live Packs. Factory Live Packs automatically unpack their contents into your Library without giving you any other options. All installed Live Packs can be viewed and uninstalled from the Preferences > Library page.
- Saving a MIDI Clip or an Audio Clip to the Library—While it is possible to save MIDI or Audio Clips to the Live Library (either through dragging a Clip into a folder in the Library via the Browser or by using the File Manager's Manage Project page), I don't recommend doing so for the following reasons:
  - If you work with your sample files in other audio programs, it is not convenient to go hunting for them inside of the Live Library's folder structure.
  - The Live Library is already a fairly large collection of files. Placing a large number of additional samples into it would make it unwieldy.
  - The Live Library is a constantly evolving database of information that is updated regularly when you install updates or make upgrades to Live, or when opening Live Packs. While it is unlikely that the Live Library would become corrupted and need to be reinstalled, it is a possibility—and for that reason I prefer to maintain a separate sample library in its own folder structure outside of the Live Library.

Backups

One final thought:

Pic. 8g: My Totem to the Impermanence of Digital Data.

I call the item in the picture above my "Totem to the Impermanence of Digital Data." Barely recognizable, it is a box of floppy disks (remember them?) that was melted in a fire that occurred at my sister's house. I don't know what was on the disks, but that is unimportant. I put it on my studio desk where I can see it every day. I use it as a reminder that no digital data is permanent. The loss of digital data is not a question of "if," but rather of "when."

I taught audio-production classes at the Art Institute of Seattle for more than a decade. Students came and went with their laptops and portable hard drives containing all their recording work. While there, a fellow instructor and friend, Tom Pfaeffle, would regularly tell his students, "Digital files do not exist unless they exist on at least three different Devices." He would then go over to the studio's DAW, open a file browser to the storage drive where students recorded their sessions, select all the files, and move them to the trash. If students had not backed up their work to their own external drives as regularly instructed to do, they would understandably panic! Tom's technique was severe, but the important lesson was painfully clear: learn to back up your data or prepare for disappointment.

Your music creations are important to you. You likely spend a great deal of time imagining, composing, arranging, mixing, and rendering them. The fruit of all this effort is nothing more than a series of ones and zeros, which are kept on some storage Device. Those storage Devices will fail (or be stolen, dropped, misplaced, eaten by the dog, caught in a fire), and when they will fail is completely unpredictable. So, your only recourse is to have some system of redundancy: storing your files in multiple places on multiple Devices. This could be a combination of computers, hard drives and DVD-Rs, ideally stored in different geographic locations. The method of making backups can be as simple as dragging-and-dropping or using a program like Apple's Time Machine.

These days, we are blessed with broadband data connections, and there are now a host of companies, such as Carbonite.com, that offer online data backup that happens seamlessly in the background. I do not rely on such a system as my only backup solution, but paired with redundancy at my home studio, it does add an additional layer of peace of mind.

Appendix A: Frequency and Amplitude

Sound is vibration. Air particles are the primary medium that acts as a carrier between the vibration source and your inner ear.

Audio is transduction, the art of turning one thing into another. Your inner ear is a transducer that turns these vibrations into electrical impulses in the brain, which you then perceive as sound.

A microphone is a transducer. Like your ear, a microphone turns vibrations into a tiny electrical current, which when amplified with a microphone preamp to a line level, can be recorded, manipulated, and ultimately amplified and sent to a speaker.

A speaker is a transducer. It takes electrical current and moves a magnetic coil that moves a speaker cone that in turn makes new vibrations in the air that your ears and brain can again transduce into sound.

An audio interface to a computer is a transducer. It takes "snapshot" measurements of electrical current and turns them into binary numbers that can be manipulated and stored. Ultimately those numbers can be transduced back into a current by your audio interface and sent to an amplifier, a speaker, the air, your ear, your brain, the world.

There are an infinite number of variables in sound and audio that affect what you hear and how you hear it. The two that you will work with the most as a manipulator of audio are frequency and amplitude.

Frequency

"Frequency" is the rate of speed, or how "frequently" something vibrates. Frequency is measured in hertz, which is a simple way of saying "number of times in a second." At a young age, the average person can perceive up to 20,000 vibrations per second, commonly referred to as 20,000 hertz (Hz) or 20 kilohertz (kHz) meaning "thousands of times per second." On the low end of the scale, somewhere around 20 Hz and below, we cease to "hear" the vibrations as sound and rather "feel" it in our bodies.

Between these two extremes, we experience frequency as pitch. Every doubling of frequency is referred to as an octave. We can hear roughly a ten-octave range of musical notes. The central frequency that we base our Western musical architecture on is 440 Hz, which translates to the note A on the musical scale. The frequency of the other A notes below "concert A" are multiple halves of 440: 220 Hz, 110 Hz, 55 Hz, and 27.5 Hz. The octaves above concert A are logically multiple doubles of 440 Hz: 880 Hz, 1,760 Hz, 3,520 Hz, 7,040 Hz, and 14,080 Hz.

In audio, any circuit or processor will change the frequency makeup of a signal to a greater or lesser degree. Quality audio gear is often known for its "transparency," which means the unit's ability to pass an audio signal with an absolute minimum of unintentional frequency change to the signal it is passing. Some Devices are said to "color" the sound passing through it, which can be an aesthetically pleasurable improvement in the sound, or a subjective diminishment. All audio Devices, from microphones to mic preamps to speakers to audio interfaces, are sought out (or passed by) for their perceived "coloration" of the sound they pass.

To intentionally manipulate the relative balance of frequencies in a recording, you use an equalizer, or EQ for short. An EQ can raise or lower the volume of specific frequency ranges to alter your perception of the material. There are several different EQ interfaces for making these frequency adjustments, such as graphic, parametric, and paragraphic EQs. But any EQ presents the user with a range of frequencies to manipulate and an adjustment for the amount of boost or cut desired. The art of EQ'ing audio is a lifelong endeavor of careful listening and exploration.

Amplitude

The other important dimension of sound and audio is known as "amplitude," and our brains experience amplitude as volume. If frequency is the measurement of the rate at which air particles vibrate, amplitude measures the amount that they vibrate. Tiny vibrations in the air might be barely audible to our ears, while an enormous volume of sound, traveling in great waves of vibration, may actually overwhelm and damage our ears.

The scale of measurement for amplitude is the decibel (dB). Essentially, the decibel is a relative measurement, meaning that it measures amplitude relative to some known, constant value. There are several different decibel reference points in audio, and as a result there are several different scales of amplitude measurement, and this is what creates a lot of the confusion about using decibels.

The second cause of confusion is that the decibel is a logarithmic scale. The dynamic range of human hearing is so vast that if you used a linear scale to measure it, you would be regularly working with values that were gigantic. Can you imagine saying to an engineer in the studio, "Would you bring the guitar down about 2,000,000 units, please?" Instead, the logarithmic nature of the decibel allows you to use much more manageable numbers, usually less than 100 in size.

A decibel reference that is fairly easy to understand is known as the Threshold of Hearing, which is the quietest sound you can perceive. The Threshold of Hearing is referenced to 0 decibels (dB) sound pressure level (SPL), or 0 dB SPL for short. Sounds louder than that are given a dB SPL value relative to the Threshold of Hearing. For example, the typical volume for a conversation between two people in a quiet environment is around 60 dB SPL, which means that the sound level is "60 decibels louder than the quietest sound you can perceive." A band in a nightclub can be as loud as 110 dB SPL. The top extreme of the dB SPL scale, known as the Threshold of Pain, is the volume at which sound becomes painful, and that is somewhere around 120 dB.

In audio, amplitude can be manipulated in a variety of ways, from a simple push of a volume fader to compressors, limiters, expanders, and gates. Any processor will change the frequency and amplitude of the signal passing through it. The question is how much, and do we like it?

APPENDIX B: DIGITAL AUDIO

As mentioned previously, in order to work with an audio signal in the digital domain—such as inside Ableton Live—the audio signal must pass through a stage of "analog to digital conversion" (or ADC) at some point. ADC is the point at which an electronic current is digitized, or "sampled," into numeric values. Later, when the digital audio is played back, the sampled numeric values must be converted back into an analog current that can be amplified and passed through a speaker. This is known as "digital to analog conversion" (or DAC). Two important variables that govern the quality, or resolution, at which these conversions takes place are known as sample rate and bit depth.

Sample Rate

When you watch a movie in the theater, you are not watching continuous motion on the screen. Instead, you are watching a series of still images that fool the brain into believing that it is watching continuous motion. These still images are displayed at 24 images (also known as frames) per second. If the rate of images per second drops below about 15 frames per second, the brain starts to be able to perceive individual still images, and is no longer fooled.

Sample rate in digital audio works in a similar fashion. Like a moving visual image in the real world, sound travels in a continuous stream and has an infinite "resolution," as does an analog audio current traveling on a wire. In order to convert this constant stream of current to into numbers that can be stored in and reproduced by a computer, your audio interface must take a series of regular amplitude measurement "pictures," known as samples. When these samples are later played back and turned back into current by your audio interface, there must be enough information, or "pictures," to fool your ear into believing that what it is hearing is a consistent flow of audio. The more samples per second taken, the greater the resolution of your audio "picture," and the more natural the audio will seem. Without enough resolution, your ear begins to hear digital artifacts interfering with the recorded signal, and is no longer "fooled.

A compact disc (CD) uses a sample rate of 44,100 samples per second. Like frequency, sample rate is expressed in hertz, or Hz, so a CD uses a sample rate of 44,100 Hz, or 44.1 kHz. This standard is considered today to be the minimum resolution for successfully "fooling" the average listener on good equipment in an ideal listening environment. Many higher-end studios today make their recordings at sample rates of 88,200 Hz (twice CD quality), 96,000 Hz (twice DVD quality of 48 kHz), or even 192,000 Hz (four times DVD quality).

Since sample rate and frequency are both measured in hertz, you may have inferred that there is some kind of relationship between the two. Without going into a lot of technical jargon, the relationship can be summed up in this way: the highest frequency that can be represented in a digital audio recording is equal to one-half the recording's sample rate. So the highest frequency that can be represented on a CD would be 22,050 Hz. That frequency is above the range of human hearing, so you might wonder, "Why would you ever need to use a higher resolution sample rate than 44,100 Hz?" That is a question of constant debate within the audio community.

Here is my take on it: All processing in the digital domain—a reverb, compressor, or EQ plug-in, or even a simple volume change—is math. A mix made in a Live Set is essentially one gigantic equation. So the primary benefit of higher sample rates is not only the increased resolution of each recording, but also the increased resolution of every math calculation made on those files from that point on, of which there are many. The same can be said for bit depth, discussed in the next section. (See appendix E, "The Makings of a Producer's Studio," for a discussion on audio-interface quality and its effect on sound quality.)

Bit Depth

We've determined that sample rate represents the rate at which your audio interface takes amplitude measurements of an incoming analog signal. Bit depth represents the resolution of each of those measurements.

If I were to ask you to tell me the value of pi in order to calculate the area of a circle, you might say "pi = 3.14." But the value of pi is actually a number of infinite resolution. You simply chose to use a resolution of two decimal points, and called it "close enough." Calculating the area of a circle using 3.14 would get you pretty close to the actual measurement, but if you used a value of pi that instead went out to 50 decimal places, you would get a much more accurate answer.

In digital audio, the resolution of amplitude measurements, or bit depth, is measured in bits. A bit is a single binary unit, meaning a one or a zero. Therefore, 16-bit amplitude measurement, which is the bit depth of a CD, might look like this: 0101110101100011 (16 ones or zeros). Counting in binary, there are 65,536 possible values between 0000000000000000 and 1111111111111111. By comparison, 24 bits yields 16,777,216 possible values, which is a significant increase in resolution.

So where sample rate correlates to frequency, bit depth correlates to amplitude. The larger the bit depth, the more dynamic range your recordings can have. Dynamic range is defined as "the difference between the loudest and softest possible sound." So, you could say that the human ear has roughly 120 dB of dynamic range. In digital, every bit represents 6 dB of dynamic range. So a 16-bit recording can have 96 dB of dynamic range and a 24-bit recording can have 144 dB. Again, a significant increase.

The digital audio measurement scale is known as "decibels (dB) below full scale (fs)," or dBfs. In digital, the reference point of 0 dB is at the top of the scale, and all other measurements are a relative negative value below zero, which represents the largest amplitude that can be measured. The reason for this is simple: in the above discussion about 16-bit resolution, there is no way to measure a value above 1111111111111111, which is known as "full scale" because all of the bits are "on." So the AES (Audio Engineering Society) standard is to make 1111111111111111 equal to 0 dB, and measure all other amplitudes relative to (and below) that. That is why all amplitude (volume) meters in digital audio use negative values.

APPENDIX C: LATENCY

In terms of digital audio, "latency" means the time it takes for audio to pass through your computer, and it is determined by your buffer size setting. You will become most aware of latency when you try to make a recording into Live and there is a noticeable delay between what you play and what you hear coming out of your headphones. If the delay you are experiencing is large enough, it can make recording a good performance impossible. Minimizing latency is a daily part of working with computers and audio, and there are several ways to go about it.

Seemingly the easiest method for minimizing latency is to lower your buffer size until the delay is small enough to not be a problem. This may work just fine for your needs. A good audio interface with well-written software drivers should have a manageably small amount of latency to begin with. And when you are recording at the early stages of a song when the complexity is low (Track counts, number of plug-ins in use, and so on), there may be little strain on your computer's resources, so a very small buffer size may be possible. But as your Sets get more complex, low buffer sizes may not be an option. What to do?

The answer lies in what is known as "external monitoring" or "hardware monitoring." Some audio interfaces have an option for this that is built in, but you can achieve much the same thing using an audio mixer. The idea is to monitor the signal you are recording before it goes into your computer. Consider these three different setups for monitoring:

Monitoring Through Live

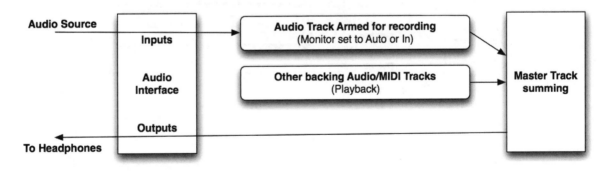

Pic. Aa: Internal Monitoring: monitoring the signal to be recorded through your computer.

- In this first picture, audio comes out of the audio interface's outputs and connects to headphones and/or speakers for monitoring. The recording Track's Monitor is set to Auto or In so that the recorded signal will be heard along with the other Tracks in Live. Since the incoming signal passes through both the input and output buffer of the audio interface before it is heard, latency is incurred. Depending on the size of the Audio Buffer setting in Audio Preferences, this delay may or may not be big enough to cause a challenge to the performer.

Hardware Monitoring

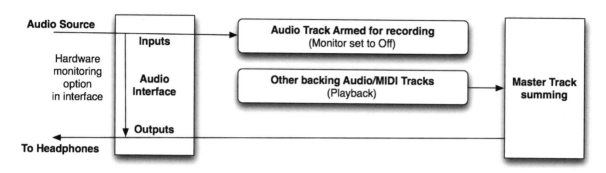

Pic. Ab: Hardware Monitoring: monitoring the signal to be recorded before it goes to the computer using the audio interface's Hardware Monitoring feature.

- In the second picture, the audio interface offers a "hardware monitoring" option that sends a copy of the incoming signal to the headphone jack (or outputs to speakers) so that the performers can monitor their performance, mixed with the backing Tracks coming out of Live. Since they are monitoring their own signal before it is digitized by the audio interface, there is no audible latency in their headphones. The input also goes to Live, where it is recorded, and the Monitor setting in Live's In/Out section would be set to Off so as not to hear a second, delayed version of the signal through the computer.

External Monitoring

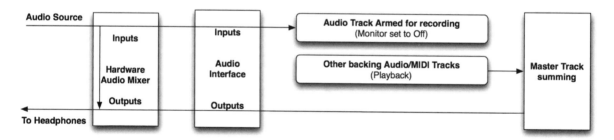

Pic. Ac: External Monitoring: monitoring the signal to be recorded before it goes to the computer.

- In the third picture, a hardware mixer is used to achieve external monitoring of sources alongside of Live's output. This provides essentially the same latency-free solution as hardware monitoring does, through an audio interface that has the added bonus of being able to mix and monitor other sources such as keyboards, drum machines, and so on, and easily incorporate external hardware processing of signals. All these items can be left plugged in, and each can be routed to the audio interface for recording via the mixer's subgroup or auxiliary buses, as desired. In this setup, all monitoring is done at the mixer, and Live's recording channels would again be set to Monitor: Off.

These three methods represent the main techniques for working with—and avoiding— latency. Consult your audio interface's manual for more advice on managing latency.

Appendix D: The Makings of a DAW

The personal computer is still a fairly recent invention. I remember when I was 12 years old and my father brought home an Apple II+, one of the first personal computers available. It had 64 kilobytes of RAM, a black-and-white 12" monitor, a 5.25" floppy drive for saving data, and a cassette drive for loading programs. It seemed like a tool of formidable power and mystery to me then, but today, the average cell phone packs more computational power than the Apple II+ had! And while working with digital audio on computers really started to become viable in the mid-1980s, the most prevalent operating systems of the day were built primarily with word processing and spreadsheets in mind. Working with audio (say nothing of video, audio's big brother) on a personal computer has always been something of a niche industry, in which you have to shoehorn the operating system into doing all kinds of things it was never originally intended to do, often at the bleeding edge of its capabilities. This situation has gotten better over the years—quite a bit better!—but it still has not yet achieved rock-solid stability. However, along with the improvement of hardware and software, computer audio enthusiasts have chiseled out some best practices for making the bumpy road less bumpy. I share some of these ideas below.

Keep in mind that in addition to Live, your controllers, and all those third-party freeware audio mangling plug-ins, your computer is your instrument! Just the way that John Coltrane knew his horn inside and out, you should get to know how your computer works intimately if you want to excel at your craft. A digital audio workstation (DAW) is a many-headed beast of great complexity. Knowing how to keep it running happily means you will spend more time making music and less time pulling your hair out.

The Computer

The overall form factors of computers these days come in many sizes, shapes, and prices. You don't need the latest and greatest computer available to make world-class music, but you do need to assess your ever-changing desires and attempt to forecast your future needs. As a regular computer user, keeping up on computer industry trends just makes common sense. Is FireWire being phased out? How fast is USB3? Are solid-state drives up to the task of a running a DAW? Keeping up with trends like these can save you money and headache when it comes time to buy or upgrade to your next computer.

Instead of shelling out top dollar for every latest and greatest computer, I try to buy "just behind the curve." By this I mean that you get the most "bang for the buck" by buying the model that was just replaced by the latest and greatest model. You have to watch for "gotchas" like hardware that is being phased out, or buying something new just before the next generation is to be released, but sometimes the "new and improved" model carries a steep price for only marginal improvements. Watch carefully, assess your needs, and be patient. My rule of thumb has been to "upgrade when a new computer comes out that has four times my current processing power." Think about that.

Laptops provide portability and are quite powerful these days, for sure. If you are a gigging DJ and can afford only one computer, a laptop is the way to go, and they can do a lot. But if you can afford and manage two, having a powerful tower as your home studio workhorse and a laptop for gigging is a killer combo. Towers are less likely to move around, get dropped, or get beer spilled on them in a club. Towers can have motherboards and peripherals that are built for serious speed. Add to that the expandability of additional internal hard drives, higher-quality optical drive burners, more RAM, PCIe cards, faster graphics cards, and multiple monitors. If you spend long hours in your studio like I do, you want a setup that is as reliable and powerful as possible. I make my music at high sample rates at home on my tower, and then render it to parts my laptop can handle for gigs. The laptop is my "stunt" computer: I will try out questionable new software on it because it is not my "mission critical" studio DAW. If the software works well, I may eventually install it on my tower. And I try not to keep anything on a laptop that I would mind losing if I left it in a taxi!

The bottom line: Reducing bottlenecks is the holy grail when it comes to DAWs. Bottlenecks are the weak links in the chain of your system that slow everything else down and prevent you from making more music. You might have the fastest, largest hard drive available, but if you do not have enough RAM, your computer may still seem slow and crash more often. Downtime is also a bottleneck. Therefore, a virus is a bottleneck. If your laptop is your only DAW, losing it means serious downtime, and that is a serious bottleneck! Your job is to find the bottlenecks and remove them as best as you can.

The CPU

The central processing unit (CPU) is the brain of your computer, and like anything you do on it, audio is just a whole lot of math. From making a 1 dB volume change to employing the fanciest linear-phase EQ or convolution reverb plug-in, it is all just math at the core. So the speed and number of your CPUs doing the heavy lifting on your system will have a great deal to do with Live's responsiveness and upper limits of capability. Thankfully, as of Live, the program takes full advantage of multiple processors, spreading the various processing jobs among them. It's like having several computers working together as one, and the improvement is significant. While some parts of your computer can get along just fine with less than the best available, this is one category in which "more is more." Buy the fastest processor you can afford. What is speedy today may be obsolete in a year or two.

The Operating System

In theory, Live runs equally well on Macs and on Windows PCs alike. I am not going to take up a lot pages and your time rehashing the age-old debate of which operating system is better. I have used both extensively, and both are quite capable. It comes down to what kind of work flow, price point, and interface makes the most sense for you. Without a doubt there is far more software (including audio software) available for a Windows machine, and that is no small thing. If geeking out on an endless sea of esoteric freeware plug-ins is your thing, Windows is the clear winner. However, if day-to-day stability, ease of use, and freedom from viruses and mal-ware is more important to you, the Mac is the clear winner ... in my humble opinion. Your mileage may vary.

Hard Drives

When it comes to DAW hardware, hard drives are a central piece of the puzzle. Having speedy and reliable access to your programs and audio data is mission critical. Thankfully, today's hard drives are bigger, less expensive, and more reliable than ever. But what do you need to do it right?

The first and easiest improvement you can make in your DAW is to have multiple drives for doing different tasks. Your operating system (OS) and the programs you run, such as Live, will access the drive they are installed on while you work just to keep the program running. At the same time, recording and playing back of audio requires almost constant access to the hard drive for retrieving the files you are working with. If you can have one drive for your OS and programs and a second drive for your audio, you will notice an improvement in speed and stability. In my computer, I take this concept one step further and have one drive for the OS and programs; a second drive for my Live Library, Loops, samples, and soft-synth Presets; and a third drive for my Live Projects and their recordings. That way I spread out the data access across three drives so that each can focus on its own task without interference, and in practice it works very well. This is one of the places that a computer tower dramatically excels beyond a laptop. Although I have seen some of the larger laptops boasting two hard drives, the additional hard drive creates additional heat and therefore requires sizeable (noisy) fans to keep them cool. But if a laptop is your only DAW, this might be a worthwhile trade-off.

When purchasing hard drives, you are striking a balance between several factors:

- Data capacity vs. cost—The cost per byte of hard-disk drives (HDDs) is on a seemingly never-ending trend of more storage for less cost. We have reached a point at which even the average drive will hold quite a bit of even high-resolution audio (while video, on the other hand, continues to grow in size and gobble up data faster than technological advances can provide it). So unless you are generating huge amounts of data on a regular basis or are working with video, there is not a great argument for buying the absolute largest drives currently available. Instead, I recommend that you buy "behind the curve," where the greatest value lies. If you divide the cost by the total capacity of the drive, you will come to a "dollars per terabyte" value and will readily find the best value. It will usually be around 75 percent of the largest drive available, in my experience. So if the largest drives available are 3 TB, look at the price per byte of the 2 or 2.5 TB drives.
- Speed of data access vs. heat generation and noise level—Here is where the average person's understanding of hard drives starts to fall off. Not all hard drives are created equal. Like cars, some are built to get you from here to there, while others are built for the autobahns of Europe! HDDs typically come in three rotational speeds: 5,400, 7,200, and 10,000 rpm (rotations per minute). A faster rotational speed means that the data on the disk can be served faster, but at the expense of more heat and higher noise coming from the drive. More heat usually means more fans to cool the computer, and thus more noise still. If you intend to record and mix audio with your computer, the amount of noise the computer makes in the room makes a big difference. You want enough speed to deliver potentially dozens of digital audio files at the same time, but you want the computer to be as quiet as possible. You get 5,400 rpm drives if you do not see a rotational speed listed with the computer, and that is typical of an office computer or basic laptop. Drives with 10,000 rpms are made for digital video and servers for which speed is of the essence and noise is not an issue. I have found that 7,200 rpm drives offer a significant performance upgrade over the 5,400 rpm drives, while not being anywhere near as noisy and hot as the 10,000 rpm drives, and so they are the way to go for either a DAW or laptop DAW. A performance 7,200 rpm SATA drive can handle over one hundred 16-bit, 44.1 kHz audio channels simultaneously, and for the home producer/laptop DJ, that should be sufficient. There are indeed other factors such as seek times (smaller is better), burst rates, and cache sizes (bigger is better), but generally speaking these statistics improve or diminish together and a good-quality 7,200 rpm performance drive that works well with your system will have what you need.
- 3.5" vs. 2.5" form factor—Hard drives come in two physical sizes. The smaller of the two, 2.5", is generally for internal laptop drives and smaller external enclosures. Their

access speeds are slower than their 3.5" cousins, so if you intend to record or play back a large amount of audio with the drive, I would encourage you toward the larger form factor. A small hard-drive enclosure may fit nicely in your pocket or laptop bag and may be fine for backing up your data, but it is not a workhorse in the way the bigger, faster drives are.

- Internal vs. external hard drives—When you need additional space for data, you may be tempted to simply plug in an external hard drive. For additional storage and backups this is a necessity, but in daily practice an internal drive will almost always be faster than an external drive, making it the better choice for your audio Project data. Additionally, how you connect an external hard drive to your system definitely makes a difference. As a rule of thumb, eSATA is faster than FireWire 800, which is faster than FireWire 400, which is faster than USB, and speed is commensurate with price. Throughput limitations will directly affect audio track counts in your DAW. An external SATA drive connected to a laptop with eSATA or FireWire 800 can be plenty fast for direct recording and playback up to its rated throughput, but USB or flash drives, while fine for portable data storage and making backups, are too slow for any serious real-time audio use. Running sample libraries directly from an external drive can be troublesome, because the access speed becomes a bottleneck. Another concern: If you have only one FireWire connection and you use that for your audio interface, then you must daisy-chain your external drive from your audio interface and they are forced to share an already narrow data channel. I've done it in a pinch, but I try to avoid it as much as possible. In short, favor internal drives when working with your audio, and use external drives to back it up.
- Solid-State Drives—In recent years, we have seen the arrival of solid-state drives (SSDs), which use a similar technology to "thumb" (flash-based) drives. They boast no moving internal parts, and therefore have much faster access times and (theoretically) fewer parts to fail. I have seen these drives in action as OS/program drives, and they are several times faster than HDDs, especially when used in laptops and when compared with 2.5" HDDs. I have seen conflicting data on their usefulness as a DAW audio playback/recording source, so the jury is still out on whether you should switch to using them exclusively. Certainly the price per byte is still quite high, but I would not be surprised to see this technology replace conventional HDDs sooner than later.
- Reliability, backups, and redundancy—Data storage of any kind, make or model, will fail. It is not a question of if; it is a question of when. And when it comes to hard drives, they either fail imperceptibly or fail completely. All of the big hard-drive makers tout their reliability, but if you check the statistics for this, they are measured in terms of "mean time before failure," which is an average lifespan of the drive before it fails. But some will fail out of the box, some on the tenth day of use, and some on the ten thousandth day of use. There is simply no way to predict when this will happen. And when a hard drive fails, the data on the drive becomes very expensive to recover. So the only antidote to this inevitability is redundancy: keeping multiple copies of all crucial data.

RAM

If the CPU is the brain of your computer and the hard drives are its long-term memory, then you can think of random access memory (RAM) as the mind of your computer, or what your computer is thinking about right now. RAM is the high-speed memory that holds the applications and documents that you have open currently. This memory is cleared when you shut the computer down, and it must be reloaded when you next restart the system. Your OS uses some RAM just to operate, as do any programs you have running. But the biggest use of RAM for DAWs are plug-ins and soft-synth instruments: the more RAM you have, the more plug-ins you can use simultaneously. Thankfully, like hard drives, RAM prices continue to plummet as the technology advances, so by all means, load your computer with as much as you can afford. More RAM means more plug-ins and fewer crashes. It's a no-brainer.

Display Monitor

While your display monitor does not directly affect sound quality in any way (unless its magnetic field is causing noise on one of your cables), the quality and size of your visual interface will dramatically affect your work flow and your amount of eye and brain fatigue. Large LCD displays are surprisingly inexpensive these days, and if you plan to spend a lot of time in your studio, do your eyes a favor and get something of large size and high quality. You ideally want to be working at a resolution at which you can see a lot and still be able to read everything easily. Your display should be placed directly between your studio speakers (also referred to as "monitors," which needlessly confuses things) in such a way as to not detract from the sound of your speakers, but still close enough to read comfortably. Live's built-in Zoom Display function in Preferences > Look Feel allows you to scale the interface to work with any screen size and resolution, and this is a tremendous benefit.

While Live's interface does not inherently support multiple displays, having two display monitors is still quite helpful: imagine running Live's interface full-screen on one monitor and all your plug-ins and Instruments on a second. Some plug-ins and Instruments can take up a lot of screen real estate. Imagine them never again obscuring your view of Live's interface, and being able to leave them open all the time on a second monitor! I've done this, and it really is a big improvement. However, I now have a 28" LCD display that fits nicely between my studio speakers, and there just isn't room for a second one unless I were to hang it above the first one from the ceiling, which I am seriously considering!

Appendix E: The Makings of a Producer's Studio

A music producer's studio is decidedly not the same as a home-recording studio, although there is a fair amount of overlap. While recording acoustic events—vocals, a bass guitar, the interesting hum of your refrigerator—could be a part of what the home producer does, the main focus often revolves around mixing elements. Those elements could be purchased samples, synthesized from instruments, "appropriated" from other recordings, or sound effects recorded in the field. Because of this fundamental shift in focus, and because more and more of the music-making work flow now happens "inside the box," the gear and space needs of the home producer have substantially shifted over the past two decades. This section attempts to identify the most relevant parameters of the space that you choose to work in, and the impact they have on your music-making experience.

The Listening Environment

I know how it is: In addition to all the "normal" things that people own and move from place to place—such as a bed, a dresser, a TV, some kitchen utensils, and clothes—you also lug around an additional set of "stuff" for making music: keyboards, speakers, drum machines, mixers, processors, and maybe a guitar or two. When you rent an apartment, it is as if you have an additional roommate, because you need a second room for all this extra stuff! At the same time, you are an aspiring musician, so perhaps you can't really afford that second room; but you need it and so you get it anyway, and this second "room" is often a hallway, a corner of a living room, or a closet. You get really creative with some furniture you found in the alley, and you manage to stack and cram all of your gear into this secondary little space. When you get it all up and running and finally get some time between your jobs to actually make music, you find yourself wondering, "Why don't my songs sound as good as (insert favorite international artist here)?"

The answer to this question has many facets, as there are many variables that affect sound quality. But the biggest two contributors to the equation (after your ears, of course) are by far what make up your listening environment:

- What are the size, shape, texture, and building materials of the space that you are listening in?
- What kind of speaker/amplification are you using, how is it placed in the room, and where are you sitting in relation to it?

These two factors are your biggest challenges when attempting to make good mixes. If you cannot clearly hear what you are trying to create, how can you know if what you are creating sounds the way you intended it?

Your Acoustic Space

Let's start with the one that is the hardest to control: the room.

The ideal listening environment has the following properties:

1. A mix room should aim to have a flat frequency response across the entire spectrum, ideally throughout the room, but at the very least, at the mix position.

A room is a resonating chamber, just like the inside of an acoustic guitar. Depending on the shape, size, and reflectivity of your listening environment, your room will naturally boost some frequencies and cut others, and these distortions, called "nodes," are your enemy. If your room, for example, naturally boosts sound waves at 100 Hz, then you will likely be unnaturally reducing the 100 Hz frequencies in your mixes (with an EQ) to make it sound "right" to you in that room. The problem is that when you take that mix to another room that is acoustically flatter, your mix will seem thin because it lacks a proper amount of 100 Hz content. In essence, you will be fighting any tonal irregularities of the room you mix in. So what room shapes create the worst nodes and should be avoided? Square rooms are the worst, and parallel walls (rectangular rooms) are the second worst. That perfectly describes 90 percent of all living spaces, doesn't it? It is a challenge, for sure. That is why the finest recording studio control rooms have no parallel walls and are designed by well-paid acousticians. What to do?

- If you are stuck using a rectangular room, situate your speakers along the short wall of any rectangle so that the speakers point into the largest space, which is behind you.
- At the same time, avoid placing your speakers directly against, or within a few feet of, a wall or ceiling. Ideally, there should be more distance between the speaker and the wall (or ceiling) than there is between you and the speaker.
- Avoid putting a speaker (or your mix position) in a corner of a room.
- Avoid flat, hard surfaces, particularly behind you. An open closet full of clothes is better than a closed closet door, for example. Having a wall of books in a bookcase is better than a flat, bare, painted drywall wall or a window.
- As a general rule, the larger the room, the better your chances of it becoming a useful mixing environment.

Cool! You can use the tone generator in Live's Audio Preferences to generate any frequency you like. When you have your room set up, turn on the tone generator and sweep the entire frequency spectrum from low to high. You should ideally hear a smooth representation of all frequencies, without any large spikes in volume at any one point. If you do, write down the frequencies and be aware of them as you mix. See if you can find a way to treat your room or move some furniture to correct the problem. Low frequencies spikes below 300 Hz will be harder to treat than higher ones.

2. A mix room should have a pleasing, natural decay, neither too short (dead), nor too long (reverberant).

If your room is highly reflective, you will likely be hearing more reflections from your walls than direct signal from the speakers, and that will cause problems. At the same time, absorbing too much of the room's natural reflectivity will leave it sounding dead and lifeless. A common myth is that putting carpet, tapestries, egg cartons, or even acoustic foam on all your flat surfaces will make a room sound better. Those materials will certainly reduce the reflectivity of some frequencies, but by no means all of them, especially the low (bass) ones. While it is possible to build or buy cylindrical bass traps to put into problem corners where bass builds up, you need to be sure that what you are doing does more good than harm. Try clapping your hands in the space: your goal is to get rid of discrete echoes and long reverb tails, but to still hear a short decay.

3. A mix room should have enough sound isolation to keep your sound from annoying others, and to keep out competing sound from outside.

This is fairly self-explanatory, but not easy to achieve. If you have the luxury of building your own space, there are many great books on how to build a room-within-a-room for sound isolation. But at the very least, choose your mix room carefully so that it meets this requirement as best as possible. Stand in the room you are considering mixing in and listen for outside noises. Walk around the building and look for neighbors who share walls in common with your mix room. Sometimes you can find a room in a building surrounded with businesses that clear out at the end of the day, which is ideal if you like to mix at night.

Monitor Placement

Aside from the rules of thumb about speaker placement above, here are the other guidelines you want follow:

4. The distance between you and your speakers should equal the distance of your speakers from each other. The two speakers and you should form an equilateral triangle.
5. Your speakers should ideally sit at ear height or just below, and be pointed directly at the mix position.
6. Avoid placing the speakers on any surface that resonates, such as a large wood table or desk. Speaker stands are best.

Speakers

The speakers you use are every bit as important as the room you put them in.

7. Your speakers should have as flat a frequency response as possible across as much of the frequency spectrum as possible when outputting a comfortable listening level.

This means that they represent all frequencies equally well, without any unnatural spikes. Speakers that seem to "feature" bass, for example, will cause you to actually lower the bass in your mixes! When selecting speakers, go to the store with one of your favorite, great-sounding CDs that you know very well, and listen to it through the various speakers they have available. You are looking for "natural" and "well balanced" more than "hyped" or "aggressive." A "comfortable listening level" is one you could work in for several hours of editing. To be specific, if you use a sound-pressure-level (SPL) meter (available at your local electronics store), it should average between 83 and 85 dB SPL, with C weighting, as you listen.

8. Your amplifier and speakers should be paired to work well with each other. An "active near-field studio monitor" is a great solution for this, as both the speaker and the amplifier are contained in the monitor and are designed to optimally work with each other.

Near-field monitors are a staple of small and home studios. Find a model that sounds good to you. Some models today even have room-analysis tools built into them to compensate for frequency irregularities.

Subwoofers

I would caution you against using a subwoofer in your studio until you know how to calibrate it properly. Two speakers can be challenging enough without adding a third that only puts out bass! Sure, it is totally sweet when the bass is thumping, but how do you know how much bass is enough?

If making good mixes is your goal, my advice to you is to use two near-field monitors only. Play a CD in a genre similar to yours that you think sounds great through the monitors, and listen carefully to exactly how much bass, mid, and high frequencies you hear. Then go mix your songs, and try to get them to sound like that CD. Keep the CD handy and repeat this process regularly to "recalibrate you ears."

Headphones

Headphones are great for keeping your neighbors and/or family happy. They also give you a second opinion of your stereo imaging and are useful when making acoustic recordings. But they are not ideal for knowing how your mix will translate to another sound system—speakers are far better for that.

Audio and MIDI Interfaces

The next most important piece of gear after your room, your speakers, and your computer is your audio/MIDI interface. It is entirely possible that you may never feel the need to make a single live recording in the process of making music. Perhaps you are a beginning producer who primarily mixes and remixes previously existing recordings. For those purposes, you may find that the headphone jack that came with your computer is sufficient for your needs. But as soon as you decide you want to start making any kind of recordings with your computer or to play out as a DJ, you will want to look at purchasing and installing an audio interface.

The first, and perhaps most important, role of an external audio interface is to get the delicate processes of analog-to-digital conversion and mic preamplification out and away from the magnetic field circus that is your computer. Spinning hard drives, power supplies, and displays all radiate significant electromagnetic fields than can create noise and distortion on your recordings. An audio interface at the end of a USB or FireWire cable is safely out of harm's way from these disturbances.

After that, the key component of an audio interface is the quality of the clock crystal that governs the timing of the samples of incoming and outgoing audio. The better the clock, the more accurately represented the recordings and playback will be through your interface. Almost any audio interface you buy today will be an improvement on the audio ports that came with your computer, and, generally speaking, you get what you pay for—and you can pay anywhere from $100 to $5,000 for a pair of stereo converters. The more you intend to record, the more you should allot in your budget for your audio interface.

In addition to quality electronic components, you are also looking for quality software drivers (the software that comes with your interface that allows you to access its features) and quality customer service. Your hardware may be amazing, but if the manual is poorly translated from another language and the control panel is buggy, you may be better off with something else.

As far as MIDI support goes, if your other gear is MIDI over USB, you may never need MIDI I/O on actual MIDI jacks. Five years ago I would have said that you needed it. Now, I am not so sure.

There are hundreds of different audio interfaces available to choose from, and they range in features and price. Some have mic preamps, some do not. Some have balanced audio connections, some unbalanced. Some have MIDI I/O in addition to audio, some do not. Some have digital inputs, some do not. Some are USB, some are FireWire. Some have more inputs than outputs, and others the opposite. You should try to imagine all the possible scenarios in which you will use your sound card, and then add a bit more functionality to grow into.

Before you buy, read as many reviews as possible and talk to others who work with audio interfaces regularly to see what they prefer. If you get on a company's support forum website and read posts from people who own the Device you are thinking about buying, you will get a great sense about the stability and compatibility of the interface, as well as a preview of what the company's customer support is like. Do a search for your computer and the interface you are considering on the manufacturer's user forum, and see what kind of experiences people have had that have a setup like the one you're thinking of buying.

Controllers

Choosing a good MIDI controller (or several) is a subjective decision-making process. In addition to doing all the same research outlined above for finding an audio interface, I can't stress enough the importance of additionally trying a MIDI controller before you buy it: features are cool, but essentially you are buying an instrument that you intend to play, so you should enjoy playing it! Go to a store that sells the piece of gear you are considering and try all of its menus, buttons, knobs, and faders. How does it feel? Does it feel musical? Does it inspire you? Does it feel well built, such that it would withstand years of use? Would the Device be easy to read and use in a dimly lit situation, such as in a club? Would the Device fit in your studio?

Mixers and Signal Routing: ITB or OOTB?

If you have several outboard pieces of gear, such as keyboards, synthesizers, samplers, effects pedals or effects Rack modules, equalizers, compressors, and so on, you will likely find yourself wanting a way to incorporate these Devices without constantly repatching all of your cables. An audio mixer or a patch bay with enough inputs to handle some or all of your Devices may streamline your work flow.

In this day and age, there are two schools of thought about mixing technique, and they are called "In the Box" and "Out of the Box."

"In the box" (or ITB) mixing is a work flow that consists of getting all your source materials digitized into the computer (or "box") and doing all mixing and processing there. The pros and cons of this approach include the following:

- Pros—All your mix automation and processing settings are saved in your Set and are instantly recallable and endlessly malleable.
- Cons—All digital processing and summing can sound somewhat harsh, brittle, and less natural than their analog equivalents, although the digital technology gets better every day.

"Out of the box" (or OOTB) mixing work flows often still use a DAW as the recording and editing medium, but mixdown happens on an outboard mixing console, with a liberal amount of outboard analog processing to boot. The pros and cons of this approach can be summed up like so:

- Pro—Take all the benefits of editing in the digital domain (cut/paste, automation) and add to that the rich, warm sound of analog processing and channel summing.
- Cons—Gear needed for working "out of the box" is many times greater in cost to own and harder to maintain. Saving your mix settings takes considerable time and effort.

Between these two extremes there is a large gray area in which producers regularly combine aspects of both ideals, utilizing some benefits of each. The modern mix environment boasts both plug-ins and select, choice hardware to accomplish specific goals. I encourage you to try both approaches as time and gear will allow.

Microphones and Preamps

Like audio interfaces and vintage outboard gear, microphones and mic preamps are sought after for their particular sound characteristics. If you don't desire to make use of acoustic recordings in your music, you may never own either of these. On the positive side, if you do want to add recordings to your sound, you can likely get away with just a few quality mics and mic preamps, or even one of each, unless you intend to Track a live drummer in your sessions, or multiple acoustic musicians simultaneously. In both cases, you definitely get what you pay for.

Microphones come in every imaginable shape, size, and cost. While there are no hard rules about what kind of microphone is used for which particular application, there are definitely trends and fashions, and the pairing of a microphone with a particular application is an art form that is developed only through many hours of experimentation. There are a number of good books on the subject that will get you started.

Mic preamps all do one difficult and delicate job: they boost a mic signal to a line-level signal. You would think that all mic preamps, having such a simple job description, would sound more or less the same, but nothing could be further from the truth. They come in many variants, such as number of mic channels, tube vs. solid state, and class of components. Some also sport built-in EQs, dynamic compression, and even analog-to-digital conversion. Some are known for their "transparency," while others are known for their "coloration" of the incoming signal.

Finding a mic and preamp combination that works for you takes a critical ear and some healthy experimentation.

APPENDIX F: THIRD-PARTY DEVICES

Once you have gotten familiar with Live's included effects and Instruments, you will no doubt be hungry for more. Thankfully, the world of third-party effects and instruments is, for all intents and purposes, endless. Over the years, a few plug-ins have floated to the surface that I use every day in my productions. I have described some of my favorites below. In my opinion, they stand out for several reasons:

- Above all, exceptional sound quality. When I hear what they do, I want to use them more.
- An innovative interface that is intuitive, easy, and fun to use. If I have to fight the interface to get the job done, I find I don't reach for it often, no matter how it might sound.
- A friendly, well-organized website and good customer service. Important when you need help or an update.

Several of these vendors have included freeware or demo installers in the downloadable book content in Book Content > Install. To install them, follow the instructions included in each respective subfolder.

Enjoy! And if you find any of these plug-ins as captivating as I do, visit their website and purchase your own copy. You will not be disappointed.

Camel Audio (www.camelaudio.com)

This company has five great products that do a lot of things simply and well. Two of these are even freeware.

- CamelPhat—A multi-effects unit that can do a number of traditional effects very well, but the addition of several unique interface options makes it exceptional. The built-in x–y assignable controller is very Ableton-esque. Like all of Camel Audio's plug-ins, CamelPhat comes with a large, rich bank of Presets, and the Camel signature Randomize button provides endless possibilities by randomizing all the controls. I've found some really "out there" sounds with the Randomizer. The plug-in has an analog-modeled compressor, three resonant filters, two LFOs, and an envelope follower. The filters and distortion are exceptional, and don't sound like any others I've used. Many plug-ins boast an analog-like "fattening" effect, but this one actually does it very well! It's hard to go wrong with CamelPhat.

Pic. TPa: The CamelPhat interface.

- CamelSpace—Similar to CamelPhat, but this multi-effects plug-in focuses on temporal effects: reverbs, delays, flanger. But what sets it apart is its Step Sequencer, which allows you to modulate several of its parameters in a fashion similar to Live's Clip Envelope. This yields some wonderful pulsing variations on whatever you feed into it. Paired with the same x-y controller and the Randomize button as CamelPhat, I never get tired of this one.
- CamelCrusher—This freeware subset of CamelPhat has distortion, compression, and a filter. Like its two big siblings above, the master section has a mix knob so that you can do some parallel processing right in the plug-in, balancing the dry signal with the wet. I am often leery of any plug-in with just one or two knobs for an entire effect, such as compression, because they are typically too limited. But CamelAudio's functions are tuned right to the sweet spot so that you can get great results fast, and from there

morph into something completely different with ease. Install this one: you will use it all the time. And it is free!

- Alchemy—Without question Camel Audio's flagship product, Alchemy is described as a "sample manipulation synthesizer." I'm just getting into this one, and the options are far deeper and wider than CamelSpace and CamelPhat combined. Alchemy is an instrument that allows you to take an audio file and play it like a sampler, but through an array of modulations. In just a short time, I've already come up with sounds that don't sound like anything I've ever heard before, so it will undoubtedly be a regular from now on. There are several multigigabyte factory patch libraries that you can download with Alchemy, and there are several more for sale.

- Alchemy Player—Alchemy Player is the free version of Alchemy, and it even comes with a 1 GB sample library! And although the controls are limited compared with Alchemy's, there is still an impressive amount of functionality here, far more than you would expect for a freeware synth—and it sounds fantastic.

Ohm Force (www.ohmforce.com)

There are companies that make plug-ins that have wacky interfaces, and companies that make excellent-sounding plug-ins, but I have found only one company that does both exceedingly well, and it is Ohm Force. This French company gives you the choice of two different skins for each plug-in: one looks quite traditional and gives you all the functionality in an elegant, compact layout, and the other . . . well, I'll let this picture speak for itself:

Pic. TPb: OhmBoyz by Ohm Force.

Yep, that is a plug-in. And an amazing one at that:

- OhmBoyz—My first Ohm Force plug-in and still a regular favorite. This plug-in is the ultimate tape-delay emulator and will put a dub vibe on anything you run through it. Up to four simultaneous delays, LFOs, filters, and an amazing distortion/saturation section. Like all of Ohm Force's plug-ins, OhmBoyz can go from subtle to lacerating, sometimes within the same Preset. I haven't found another delay plug-in that can do what this one does, nor have I even been able to re-create its sound with an Audio Effect Rack and a dozen other plug-ins. Highly recommended.

- Quad Frohmage—There are boring filter plug-ins, and then there are plug-ins that make you instantly sound like a superstar. Quad Frohmage is the latter. There are four concurrent resonant filters that sound amazing, each with LFOs, delays, and distortion. Different routings allow the filters to feed each other or to happen in parallel. If you make electronic music, get this right now!

- Frohmage—This is the freeware version of Quad Frohmage, and as the name implies, it has only one filter, but it is one amazing filter and it is free! Try this one, and if you love it like I do, buy Quad Frohmage.

- Ohmicide:Melohman—Again, there are distortion and amp simulators, and then there is Ohmicide:Melohman. If you have heard an overdriven guitar amp feed back on itself, or just about to, you've heard what this plug-in is all about. Most digital distortion plug-ins sound grainy, thin and harsh, but this one sounds warm, fuzzy, and pleasing. And by pleasing, I mean nasty! This is the only distortion plug-in that I know of that feeds back on itself in such a convincing way. From subtle tube warmth to obliterating mayhem, Ohmicide:Melohman does it all. Perhaps its most unique feature is the ability to morph between Presets, which is mind-bending to behold. If you make breaks, dubstep, or drum 'n' bass, this has you all over it. Try this on anything, even an entire mix.

- Hematohm and Mobilohm—Both of these cover phase-, flanger-, frequency-shift-type effects, but like all of Ohm Force's plug-ins, they have a warm, saturated, analog feel that is so rare in plug-ins. Add a little sparkle or descend into 1970s sci-fi madness. File under exotic and delicious.

Spectrasonics Omnisphere (www.spectrasonics.net)

Pic. TPc: Spectrasonics Omnisphere interface.

Most plug-in instruments are niche synths that do one or two things well. If you want the end-all-be-all synth, look no further. I would vote for Omnisphere for both "Best-Sounding Synth" and "Best All-Around Synth," and that is saying a lot: those are two big and important categories.

As far as sound quality goes, "big" and "clean" are be the words that best describe this product. Crystal-clear highs, big round lows, and zero mud. Where OhmForce was a warm, grainy maelstrom, Spectrasonic's synths are cool, crisp, watery, and clear. When you are making ambient, downtempo, progressive house, trance, or other genres in which depth and clarity are essential, this is a synth to reach for. The built-in effects are immersive and clean, so you may not need additional processing afterward. Each Preset you bring up is a fully formed world awaiting your complete immersion.

Omnisphere is often referred to as a "rompler," which is a synth/sampler that plays back from a large library of samples. As far as Preset sounds go, this one comes with a 50 GB sound library on six double-layer DVDs. If you have the hard-drive space, this is one formidable arsenal. It boasts more than 1,000 Presets, all tagged and sortable by keywords. There are multiple editing layers to be had here as well, so the process of creating your own sounds can go as deep as you desire.

Omnisphere's brilliance requires a CPU that can do the required heavy lifting. Be sure to check the system requirements before you take the plunge of purchasing it. Because of the gigantic sample library, Spectrasonics does not offer a demo version, but the company's website contains a nice bevy of videos that feature the product in a realistic way. Check it out.

TAL (http://kunz.corrupt.ch)

TAL stands for Togu Audio Line, and is the brainchild of Patrick Kunz. As far as donationware goes, Kunz is turning out some great stuff. Aside from his creative array of audio plug-ins, what drew me to his work were his soft-synth instruments, the Elek7ro II in particular. (No, that's not a typo—the name really has a 7 in it!) For a donation of your choosing, this little synth is light on your resources and packs a punch. A basic set of controls provides an impressive range of sounds and is perfect for someone just getting into synthesis. In this book's companion book, Sound Design, Mixing, and Mastering with Ableton Live, I show you how to stack a few of these using an Instrument Rack. If you are just getting going and aren't ready to throw down for Omnisphere, give these a try.

Pic. TPd: The TAL Elek7ro II soft synth.

Voxengo (www.voxengo.com)

I have to admit, I am a little late to the party on this one, but I went looking for a freeware Peak/RMS/K-System master meter for use in the follow-up book, which has a section on mastering. Many reviewers said that Voxengo SPAN was not only free but had replaced their other paid-for meters in daily use. I've been using it for a few months now, and I really like it. Beyond that, Voxengo has a wealth of other plug-ins, all in VST/AU format, and they sound great. They lean toward the more technical, audio-engineering side of things, but I've already gotten some very creative sounds from them. More on these plug-ins in the second book.

Pic. TPe: Voxengo SPAN master meter.

Appendix G: How to Use the DVD Content

The included DVD contains many useful files for your enjoyment. This appendix will walk you through the steps for making the most of them.

1. Begin by inserting the DVD into your computer's DVD-ROM drive. When the DVD icon shows up in your file browser—Finder on Mac, Windows Explorer on PC—double-click it to see its contents. You should see a single folder named Book Content.
2. Click and drag the Book Content folder to your Desktop. Many of the included files will need to be modified as you work with them, and DVDs are a read-only storage medium. Having a copy on your Desktop will allow you quick, easy access to the content, as well as providing you modifiable versions of the files.
3. When the files are done copying to your Desktop—the content is roughly 623MB in size—navigate to this new copy of Book Content on your desktop and open it. You should see the following three folders inside:

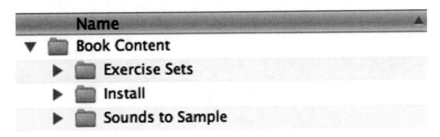

Pic. Ad, Contents of the Book Content folder (Mac)

The three subfolders contain the following:

- Exercise Sets—This folder contains all the Ableton Live Sets that correspond to each exercise in each chapter. They are in Project subfolders divided by chapters. If you want to simply start at the beginning of chapter 1 and follow along with each exercise sequentially, you will likely not need these Sets, as each exercise picks up right where the previous exercise left off—you can easily complete the entire book's exercises in this linear manner. But should you desire to double-check your work against mine, or jump ahead a few exercises, these sets are here to allow you that flexibility. As I detail at the beginning of each exercise in the book, my recommendation is to immediately perform a Save As command after opening one of these Sets, resaving the set in the same Project folder with a new name of your choosing so that you still have the original Set to reopen should you need or want to. Of course you still have the DVD with unalterable originals of all these Sets should you accidentally modify and save over any of these Sets—you could simply recopy a Set from the original DVD to your Book Content folder on the Desktop at any time should you need to.

- Install—The second folder is a collection of third-party plug-ins that can be used within Live to broaden your sonic palette. These are each described briefly in the previous appendix to help you decide if they would be interesting to you. Some are freeware/ donationware—meaning you may install and use them without restriction, and the author hopes that, should you decide to keep using the software, you might consider visiting their websites and making a donation for their continuing efforts—or demo versions of paid-for products that will cease to function after an introductory time has elapsed. In order to use these plug-ins, open the subfolder (Mac/PC) that pertains to your operating system, then navigate to the installer of the plug-in you want to install, double-click it, and follow the onscreen instructions. The only plug-in that does not work this way is the TAL-Elek7ro-II VST, which has no installer application and needs manual installation. The TAL-ReadMe.txt file in the TAL folder will walk you through this manual installation process of copying the .vst file to the proper system folder. Visit the plug-in vendor's website for more information about purchasing a full version of a plug-in you like, or how to uninstall a plug-in you don't like.

- Sounds to Sample—This folder contains an assortment of audio files from SoundstoSample.com for use with the book's exercises, sorted into subfolders by type. During the exercises, I will instruct you to navigate into these subfolders regularly using Live's built-in Browser. You will not use every file in every subfolder in the exercises, so feel free to experiment with any/all of them on your own. They are yours to use in any way you like, royalty- and restriction-free. I highly encourage you to visit SoundstoSample.com for more raw audio materials. They have an extremely large selection of samples across a large range of sonic genres to choose from at a competitive price.

That is a lot of content to work with and should keep you busy for days and weeks to come. And yet we have only scratched the surface of what is possible and available in the vast world of Ableton Live. I wish you the best of luck in your sonic endeavors.

INDEX